JUST IN TIME

How   *)y and*
Synchroni   *:ry Moment*

KAR   ROSE
CALLAN

ISBN: 1482705648
ISBN-13: 9781482705645
Library of Congress Control Number: 2013904630
CreateSpace Independent Publishing Platform
North Charleston, South Carolina

***

for grandma

***

INTRODUCTION

I stretch people. Not only in the physical sense as a yoga teacher, but in emotional, behavioral, and spiritual senses as well. I do so for just one reason—Joy.

I believe life is meant to be joyful. I believe that God and the entire Universe are here to support us through this venturesome time of great growth and healing. I believe that we are the only ones standing in the way of living in complete awe and daily gratitude for all of our experiences. And I believe that being open and accepting of life as a mystery can bring us to a level of experience we could never fully imagine: a space where tears flow from a moved heart and chills rise with visions of possibility.

Today, I invite you to join me on a journey: two spirits traveling through time, still connected. May it move you with encouragement and zeal to enjoy life, to live fully, and to love. May you explore new ideas and insights, bringing you to a personal peace and love of yourself. May you also come to spiritually recognize when "it is time" to just be, to get going, to wade through, or to move over and allow the universe to guide you with ease and laughter on your passage.

I know Grandma would be pleased in getting to know you, as you experience her life through story, music, and signs. She loved life and wanted others to love it as well—a life with no beginning and no end.

ACKNOWLEDGMENTS

I am extremely grateful to all of the spiritual teachers who have deepened my faith, shared their wisdom, told their stories, and offered their talents. To be walking on this Earth with them and enjoying this God-given life is an honor and much greater than I could have ever imagined.

To my grandparents, Rosa and Walter Moore, Fred and Josephine Kalil, Grandma Eva, and Grandma Jere, thank you. I feel so blessed to have been given such a rich, fruitful background. You were, and still are, the wisest people I know. Thank you for instilling in me great morals and nurturing my strong faith. I appreciate you more than words can express and think of you often with great love and admiration.

For being such wonderful and caring parents, I thank my mom, Judi, and my dad, Frank. You always encouraged me to try new things, took me places I had never been, and gave me opportunities I hadn't thought possible. Thank you for creating a space to learn and grow and for loving me fully.

To my husband, Kelly, whose constant support and devotion continue to inspire and amaze me. You are my best friend, my partner, and my rock of thirty one years. You have been a patient, kind witness to my ever-changing interests, and I am thrilled that we are on this journey together. You're the best. I love you.

And finally, to my children: my daughter Kimberly and her husband Jason, my daughter Kristina and her husband Levi, my son Christopher, and my daughter Courtney. My heart swells with joy at being the one you call "Mom." You demonstrate all that is well in this world, with your acts of kindness and love toward one another and those around you. I feel blessed every moment I share your company. Thank you for laughing at my puns, putting up with my *creative* recipes, and supporting me on this wild ride. But more than that, thank you for spending your time with me. I couldn't be happier.

When we aren't able to stay closely connected with our blood relatives, we consider others as "family" in their places: best friends and neighbors, coworkers and teachers, dogs and cats. All are felt with that same expression of "loved ones." I am blessed to be surrounded by so many. Thank you.

My husband, Kelly, jokingly tells people, "The color of Karen's sky is a little different than everyone else's." He's right. It is. But it sure looks a lot like heaven.

Part 1
HERE'S ROSE

TIME–

What is time?

We count it in seconds, minutes, hours, and days,

but the universe doesn't count time.

A child's life of fifteen days and a person's life of eighty-five years—

each is a lifetime to the Universe.

One means neither less nor more than the other.

Both make an impact on the world, and both have a profound purpose.

1

JUST IN TIME

Grandma Moore saw everyone as one race—human.

Her magnetism was obvious. An attention-giver and attention-getter, Grandma was the ultimate people person. Relating, conversing, enamoring, assisting, instructing, discovering…Grandma was a brilliant communicator and thrived on people's energies. *"Rosa Gemma Brunorini Scarlatti Moore."* She always pronounced her *full* name with pride and lyrical inflection. Engaging in a conversation with Grandma was like watching a symphony conducted by Beethoven. With each syllable, her fingers fluttered through the air. Hands waved. Arms lifted. She charmed everyone with her boldly gregarious comments and fun-loving vigor. Grandma knew no other way to be.

Whenever I was in her company, there was always the anticipation of "What will she do next?" Like when she directed my grade school friend into the bathroom and, without missing a beat, pulled out her full set of dentures, leaving nothing but her wrinkled lips and exposed gums. This was followed by her "Use floss or this will happen to you" talk. Or when, on command, she squeezed her upper arm and belched. Yes, this was quite the trick. Her familiarity with her lymphatic system proved useful in flatulent situations. She willingly shared anything and everything that was less than pretty or positive, if it would help save someone future pain.

I grew up fascinated by her high energy, her ability to speak her mind, and her willingness to communicate and share personal information. Countless people were drawn to her liveliness, but for some adults, she was a nuisance. She asked candid questions, entered personal spaces, and at times acted childish with her persuasive voice and dramatic behavior. Admittedly, her direct approach caused some negative reactions, but her intent never wavered from love.

Grandma once held me and said, "Our hearts are one. We are *simpatico*." She had a lot of love to give, and I had a lot of love to get. Our relationship worked perfectly.

There can be something extra special about a grandma— a universal figure representing absolute love. From a child's perspective, the care and nurturing received from a grandmother is boundless. Her wisdom and pure heart can be the greatest single contributor to a child's happiness.

I arrived from the Kansas City Airport and hurried down the long white tiled hallway to the eight-hundred wing. The moment I walked into the pale yellow hospital room and saw Grandma Moore, I knew. She couldn't speak, but she looked directly at me with piercing eyes, suggesting more than just "hello." I quickly leaned in to hug her as she reached out for me, squeezing my hand so tightly it throbbed. In my mind I heard, "Let me go." Over and over again, the depths of her silent voice pleaded loud and clear, "Let me go! Let me go!" I looked back at my mom and shared the message with her. We both agreed that it was not right to prolong her suffering. Her physical body was shutting down, and although she was an enthusiast of life, she was ready to pass.

Grandma Rose always said she wanted to "make it to ninety." She had been ill on and off for the past year. Just three weeks after her ninetieth birthday, she was admitted into the hospital, her last stay.

My older sister, Jo Ann, flew in later that evening and joined us at the hospital as we kept vigil over Grandma. During the last few years, the three of us had each spent our fair share of energy and time, driving her to appointments and taking her on lunch outings—each excursion a probable adventure. Memories and stories from our recent past flooded in. "Remember when I took Grandma to lunch at The Eclectic Café with Tyler, when he was two?" Jo, as she liked to be called, reminisced. "They *both* ordered off of the kids menu. And the nicest waiter walked over to Jack in the Box to buy her French fries to go with her grilled cheese sandwich, since they didn't make them."

I added, "Or how about the time when she was living with us?" My sweet husband, Kelly, offered to have Grandma move in with us a few years earlier, after she suffered a mini-stroke and needed to move out of her San Francisco apartment. "Remember when Kelly brought her a glass of water with ice in it? 'What?' Grandma said, 'Are you trying to kill me?'" Her darting words flew across our kitchen table as she reminded us that she *never* drank cold water, due to the strain it put on her digestive system.

Now quiet, Grandma simply lay still. Her eyelids closed and her time of responding ended as she melded into a deep, restful state. A sense of peace seeped into the room. Sitting, standing, leaning, and waiting - the nurse urged us to go home and rest and said she'd call if there were any changes, adding, "These things take time."

We arrived first thing the next morning with music, books, and magazines in hand. Mom said, "Karen, why don't you pick out some music to listen to, so we don't have to hear all the noise from the nurse's station?" Knowing that Grandma would not be leaving her room, we made the space as intimate and homey as possible.

I chose *Broadway's Greatest Hits*, a musical compilation of original soundtracks, and pressed play. "Oh, What a Beautiful Mornin'" chimed its musical notes, mimicking a gentle bird call as the early sun emerged. We arranged the chairs around Grandma's bed and settled in for the day.

Songs with harmonious, uplifting messages continued, from "On the Street Where You Live" to "New York, New York" to "Put on a Happy Face," shielding our room from the sounds of beeping machines and clamoring voices. Bold, hopeful, and passionate, each lyric highlighted a different facet of Grandma's character.

A nurse entered, counting numbers of heartbeats and breaths. We followed her with our eyes as she took Grandma's pulse, checked her IV, and walked out. Making arrangements with relatives on the phone, Mom stood off to the side of the room. Jo and I looked at Grandma's face. Her breathing was now shallow and slow, with longer pauses in between. We then looked at each other, and took deep breaths of our own, as if to make up for the one Grandma couldn't take. "Mom, you need to get off of the phone," I said bluntly. "It's time."

"Let me call you back." Mom immediately hung up, and moved to the top of the bed, and began stroking Grandma's forehead. Jo and I stepped closer to her sides, shielding her from whatever wasn't sacred. "It's OK, Mom. You can go," she said, as she swept her fingers through Grandma's hair. All of us centered and focused on Grandma.

"Just in time…" Lyrics floated through the air. "You found me just in time. Before you came, my time was running low. Now you're here, and now I know just where I'm going, no more doubt or fear. I'm on my waaaaayyyy."

And she died.

The lyrics continued, "For love came just in time, and changed my lonely life that lovely day."

Instantly, the room became eerily still. The song ended. Silence ensued as one long teardrop rolled down Grandma's cheek. Jo wiped it away with a loving sigh, "She's sad to go." And then the next song rang in.

"Wherever we go, whatever we do, we're gonna go through it together. We may not go far, but sure as a star, wherever we are, it's together. Wherever I go, I know *he* goes."

"Listen," I said. "She must be seeing Grandpa right now." He, her husband of sixty-four years, had passed four years prior. I imagined them embracing, both ecstatic to see each other.

"Wherever I go, I know *she* goes…"

It felt as though Grandma sent us a reaffirming message: "I'll be with you as well." "Amigos, together." As we laughed through our tears, the musical tribute carried on, lifting us out of time and into a space of wonder. We stayed in our family cocoon and listened. Each song became a cherished gift of hidden treasure. Life loved Grandma, and she loved life. And true to her nature, she passed on with a chorus line of hits and stars. If it were possible to write a script for her departure, this would surely have been hers.

keeping her spirit alive

I was raised on musicals. *Camelot, West Side Story, Funny Girl*...they all filled my childhood home. As a kid, Mom let me play her albums in the living room whenever I wanted, dancing and choreographing one-girl shows for her to see. The hearth of the fireplace became my makeshift stage, which doubled as a jumping-off point for the crescendos. As soon as I felt "the show" was ready for an audience, I would run through the house to find her. "Mom! Mom!" I'd shout as I raced around the corner. Mom would sit down on our green velvet plush sofa holding her dish towel or dust rag, as I often dragged her away from whatever cleaning project she was tackling. I sang. I danced. She clapped.

Any chance Mom and I had to listen to musicals, we took. We loved everything Broadway. As I grew older, I made it a point to stay up to date with current productions.

And then this happened.

When the song "Just In Time" played on the day of Grandma's passing, it was the first time I had ever heard it. It shocked me that on a disc titled *Broadway's Greatest Hits*, there existed a song I had never listened to before. I've seen numerous local productions, national touring shows, and shows on Broadway and London. I had what I thought to be a wide ranged collection of Playbills and CDs. Yet, here was this song!

After Grandma died, I went back and listened to the entire disc as a way of connecting to and revisiting the experience of her passing day. Each tune became a source of healing and strength, as I began life without Grandma. The music embodied her fun-loving and energetic spirit. As I relived those pure, precious moments, I gained clarity about the significance of the song's meaningful words.

"Just in time." I played the song over and over again, memorizing the lyrics and repeating the melody. "Just in time," I sang while driving to work. And then it hit me. True, we arrived the day before she died. True, we were there by her side as she passed. But it wasn't that we had barely made it or that our time was short. It also didn't convey that we almost missed an important happening. Just in time meant just—*in*—time.

It was how Grandma lived—Just *in* Time!

She wasn't stuck in the past or worried about the future. She squeezed all the juice out of life and lived for every instant, centered on being present. "You found me just in time." Anyone who knew her knew she didn't miss a beat.

In the divine arena, I wondered if "Just In Time" had been planned for me, anchoring in the profound moments of her death. Was that even possible, to orchestrate the perfect passing at the perfect instant for this song to be heard? Could her soul have requested that? Or my soul, for that matter? And if so, how many other souls were involved in this truly remarkable arrangement?

I am not sure.

But I do believe that keeping an open mind enhances my life experience. Not having all the answers or explanations allows me to stay in a state of awe. I am always on the lookout for the unknown, the unexplained, and the unexpressed. With each journey comes new understanding and a new reason not to understand anything at all.

My goal is to simply enjoy the possibilities. Because I believe God is connected to all that takes place, in and around me, I see each and every happening as a sign. The people I encounter, the songs on the radio, the thoughts and dreams that come to mind… each of these are a message, a clue to pay attention to.

To this day, if I am ever out and I hear "Just In Time" playing, I think of it as a "*Ciao*" from Grandma. And if someone uses the phrase "just in time," again, for me, it's a sign. "Grandma's here," I always say out loud. In line at the Wild Animal Park—Grandma. At the outdoor mall playing over the speakers—Grandma. Sitting in a restaurant with Jo and overhearing a couple's conversation at the table behind us—Grandma.

Keeping her spirit alive—me.

I'm listening…

It didn't even occur to me until later that the song "Together Wherever We Go" from the musical *Gypsy* is sung by the strong feminine lead character, Rose. Of course!

2
THE PRACTICE
OF YOGA

One Saturday morning, at the age of five, I woke up and, still in my pajamas, walked in on Grandma, who was upside down, practicing her headstand. "Hi, honey," she said. Grandma towered out of the floor like an inverted statue in the middle of the room. Her feet dangled above the edge of her pant legs. She had no problem talking, even when she was upside down. "How did you sleep?" That's just like Grandma, keeping up with a conversation, even on her head.

Grandma lowered one leg after the other and sat up on her knees. She always looked exactly the same to me, from when I was little until shortly before she died. Her natural grey hair hung straight in a short bob, about chin length, with wispy bangs hanging on her forehead. A creamy shade of light brown, her eyes were wide, bright, and focused.

"Come here and get on the floor with me," she said as she patted the carpet. Thin and flexible, her arms and legs were always in motion. Together we reached and stretched, twisted and lengthened, inhaled and exhaled. "You always learn something new about yourself," she said, as she placed her hands on my shoulders, drawing them back while supporting my spine.

Back in the forties, when Grandma started practicing yoga, very few people talked about it or even knew what it was; and if they did, the words "strange" or "out there" usually found their way into the conversation. Grandma developed her yogic lifestyle independently. No classes were offered in convenient studios. There was no one for sharing insights, discoveries, or inquiries. No in-depth writings or images published, only a few basic handbooks and pamphlets. But thanks to a public television show, Grandma became the completely dedicated student of just one teacher—Lilias.

Every day of every week, Grandma practiced yoga on her living room floor while watching "Lilias, Yoga and You." Just like a dear friend next door, Lilias Folan was a voice of encouragement, a model of well-being, and a trusted teacher. For years, her gentle ways and easy approach were like oxygen to Grandma and others like her.

During those memorable times while growing up, I sat mesmerized as I watched Grandma practice. I couldn't believe how effortlessly she moved. Inversions, bends, compressions… she and her yoga were one. And that's how it was.

Her fifty-year dedication became her saving grace, keeping her from many of the physical and emotional hurdles that plagued others. I still remember the day Grandma called after tripping over a street curb while walking home in San Francisco. At eighty-five, she was obviously shaken up by the fall, yet she was ecstatic that she hadn't shattered a single bone. "I am the only person I know who hasn't broken a wrist after falling," she declared. "And that's because of my *yoga*!"

Like any great news with Grandma, her story of how yoga saved her was communicated repeatedly in hopes of saving another body from needless suffering. If it was worth sharing once, it was worth sharing twice more, she believed. She blessed yoga and Lilias every day for her strong bones and steady self. She now stepped even more carefully and thoughtfully than before.

On the occasions when we walked around her Marina neighborhood, we'd say "Hello" and give hugs to friends who were older *and younger* than she. After walking away, Grandma would lean in and say, "I'm getting taller, and everyone around me is shrinking." We met one younger, hunched-over friend with obvious osteoporosis and arthritis. She shared the story of her ailments as Grandma and I leaned in and listened. Her sweet smile, hiding the obvious pain in her joints. We hugged and said our good-byes. After walking away Grandma whispered, "Poor thing. She's had such a tough time." Grandma then sprinted away, as I ran to catch up to her.

continuing the yoga tradition

Although I enjoyed yoga with Grandma and also enjoyed attending the occasional class, I didn't make yoga a habit until after she died. Like most people, getting into a regular yoga routine was a choice I made after a less-than-positive medical appointment.

The doctor told me that adding a consistent form of exercise could possibly stave off the irregular painful symptoms of my monthly moon cycle and strongly suggested that I incorporate exercise into my daily routine.

After three different friends suggested yoga, I started my practice. And yoga worked! I loved how I could breathe with a full set of lungs. I loved the energy I could build and create and ignite. And I loved moving in synchronicity with all the various aspects of my self and my breath.

With my new practice came a contentment and recovery that stunned not only me but all those around me. "You look so healthy. What are you doing?" people would ask. I told them of the balance and healing I had recently experienced with yoga and of how various symptoms I had accepted for years were now gone.

"How do you stay looking so young?" they would add. "Yoga," I answered. And that was it. The strength, peace, and lightheartedness I gained from yoga were the real reasons for my vibrancy. True, the physical activity helped my aches disappear, but now my heart sang with good health. Because of this, people asked me to teach. So I taught.

For me, yoga is gratitude in motion.

Each day, I consciously walk and work with a body of thankful energy. I mindfully allow my gratitude to swim through and emanate out of me. It is the first sentiment I express each morning when I wake up and the last feeling I convey each night before I sleep. Sensations of complete appreciation dictate my day. I say:

"Thank you, God, for all of my blessings. Thank you
for using me today to be of service. Thank you for guiding

me to be where I need to be, to say what I need to say, and to do what needs to be done. Thank you for all of my abundance and for all of my blessings. I am truly grateful."

With thankfulness, I channel the energy in the yoga studio, asking the angels to come and assist me, guiding me with the words, messages, and positions my students need that day. Once I give in to outside help, I am able to relinquish control, confident that the right phrases and movements will present themselves. From one pose to the next, I trust, having no idea what's coming up next. Each moment—a pure act of faith.

Significant expressions, clear images, extraordinary glimpses. The body goes from feeling tight, heavy, overworked, messy, and argumentative to open, supple, free, relaxed, and strong. Wrinkles soften, stresses exit, and struggles release.

My teaching takes me to many diverse places. I have observed anger melt away from troubled teens as I gently spoke words of encouragement to them just outside the cells of their juvenile detention center. I have watched rambunctious preschoolers become quiet, still, and focused. I have seen a bride's nervous butterflies settle into calm confidence on her wedding day. I have witnessed many of my students transform into more secure, genuine, peaceful, and influential human beings.

During class, I actually see the state of bliss move into my students' energy fields and take over; their eyes becoming open channels to their souls. Because of this, at times I teach with my eyes closed. There is something so extraordinary about the practice that, once heaven moves in, I feel as though I am imposing if

I watch. So I take short gazes, remaining connected, yet not crossing the line of what is meant to stay sacred.

together at last

A few years ago, I took a long-awaited weekend workshop here in Tucson with Lilias. I walked into the large space and laid out my mat along with the sixty or so others who obviously knew they were in for a treat. We listened and learned about the various nuances and subtle changes the body feels in the poses. During the practice, I heard Grandma's voice speak through her: "Exhale slowly and smoothly." The entire class felt like home, with a tangible connection to those early days, with Grandma on our living room floor. "Tears are our birthright. The purpose of yoga is to know thyself. If thyself is having a moment of shimmering depression, let's look at it, then let it go." There were certain moments when Lilias spoke, when I actually believed it *was* Grandma.

At the end of class, I patiently waited while other students finished their thankful good-byes. My heart raced and my stomach swirled as I approached the woman I had heard about for so many years. I was about to meet Lilias.

Eagerly, I stepped forward and asked her to please be in a photo with me. She quickly obliged. I looked at her familiar face and brown wavy hair. She was curvier and taller than I had imagined. She oozed a beautiful kindness that felt like a warm blanket. Breathing in the moment, I shared the story of exactly how great an impact she'd had on Grandma's life and now on mine. I told her of Grandma's great dedication and the complete joy she felt while watching her show on PBS for so many years. I shared all of the love and gratitude that Grandma would have personally liked to have passed on, as I held back tears of pent-up anticipation and appreciation.

Lilias smiled, squeezed me, and held me close. "Please, please. Let's take another picture." We leaned our heads in toward one another. "I would love for you to bring a photograph of Grandma Rose to put on the altar tomorrow. It would be wonderful to have her presence here."

The next day, before our practice began, Lilias introduced Grandma to the community, saying, "Rose inspired many people in her life, and we are blessed to have her with us today." A framed photo of Grandma sat humbly alongside the photos of Lilias's teachers. Each time we twisted and stretched, I smiled. I could see Grandma smiling at the group from her photo and felt her happiness of being there. Through me, Grandma had finally met her special, dear Lilias. And Lilias got to meet her, too.

Lilias Folan and I, together at last.

why? because i can

A few years ago, I adopted a new affirmation: "Because I Can." When people asked me, "Why do you practice and teach nine classes of yoga a week?" I responded, "Because I can."

"Why do you still volunteer when you don't need to?"

"Because I can."

"Why do you do all of those things that others could do for you?"

"Why not? Because I can."

Ask anyone midpose in my yoga class the answer to my question of "Why?" And ringing through the air in unison you'll hear, "Because we can!"

I have three friends in my life who have adapted to spending time in wheelchairs. All of them were changed by some human accident. When I see what their days include and what skills they use, I not only admire their capability and talents, but I feel less like complaining and making excuses. And yet, so many of us throw our gifts away. If there is a physical, mental, or emotional reason why we can't do a particular thing, well, that's another story. But for many of us, we can.

We can bend and reach and help and change. We can write and touch and dream and pray. We can listen and speak and taste and see. We can sense and discover and study and grow. We can do so much and be so amazing.

Last year I was on a trip, visiting a friend. While waiting at the airport, I pulled out my CD case and headphones and flipped through the variety of music genres and albums. Inside, I noticed one blank disk. Out of curiosity, I loaded it in my player and pressed play.

"Because we can can can. Yes, we can can can. Yes, we can can can can can can can can!" From the movie *Moulin Rouge,* my mantra repeated vociferously, over and over again.

"Everybody can can!"

My sentiments exactly.

3

LIVE AND LET LOVE

"*Oh, amore,*" Grandma whispered while placing her open hands over her heart with an affectionate Italian gesture. I remember her immediate acknowledgment of joy when she witnessed love budding. While watching a couple holding hands or locked in an embrace, she would stop, close her eyes, and draw their world into her own, each time filling the well for her own capacity to love.

Grandma once told me that we were both the same. We were both lovers of life. I admittedly struggled with that concept, when life's challenges overwhelmed me, but she made loving look easy. It was her effortless expression of affection that I marveled at—to be able to touch others just for the sake of connecting and hug strangers without concern about appearances or comfort levels.

Grandma took any opportunity to get close to another person. If you were standing near enough, your arm was fair game for rubbing as she looked into your eyes and spoke directly to you. Up and down, her hand would stroke your skin. And this was true even if your sleeve was longer than she liked.

"*Ciao bella!* How was your day?" she would ask me, as she reached under my sleeve, moving higher for more contact. "*Simpatico…*" she would add, as her fingers combed my hair, sweeping it back behind my ears. Before I knew it, I would fall into a hypnotic state of "Grandma love."

Growing up in a family where showing affection was reserved for holidays only, I couldn't wait to be with Grandma. Her signature style of wrapping me up in her arms helped me forget about the detachment I felt within my own family. She held me till I was full again, and then she passed me on to Grandpa for more.

Her expressive love was especially contagious to me, a young girl, who wanted to show affection but struggled in doing so. Many times, I felt constricted by my own words or actions. I longed to speak up yet stopped myself before expressing my true feelings. It took me years to get through the awkward "hello hug" to my brother and the muddled sign-off "I love you," on the phone to my sister. Thankfully, I didn't give up. After many uncomfortable and tongue-tied moments in the beginning, they both responded with the same desire to exchange affection.

In fact, Grandma started a wave of affection through me, and I now offer it freely and without pause, as does my entire family. And although I give credit to Grandma for the ability to share the abundance of love in my life, it was no secret that her love stemmed from faith and gratitude. Grandma always gave credit to God. For those of us within reach, kisses flew in all directions. Bursting, humming, smacking. Her kisses were multiple, extravagant, and loud, whether traveling through the air or planted on a cheek. And anyone not within close proximity received regular sounds of her love by phone or letter. *"Te amo, Te amo. xo xo xo."* If there was anything greater than her drive to enjoy life, it was love. Love. Love. Love.

love yourself

Grandma loved herself fully. Not in a vain way; she simply loved her life, her breath, her body, and her voice. She was the center of her attention. She never conformed to who others wanted her to be. She really didn't care what other people thought of her, and I really didn't care what other people thought of her, either. Her imperfect ways gave me the freedom to let go of my perfectionist nature. She had flaws and rough edges. She stepped into your personal space and spoke out of turn. She was blunt, loud, and demanding when necessary, yet didn't seem to be afraid of anyone or anything. She just always showed up as herself.

"Live and let love," was Grandma's motto. At any time or in any situation, love directed the action and the outcome. And each opportunity that presented itself was an opportunity to love. Whether she loved the artist, the neighbor, the foreigner, or the relative, loving others and herself took center stage in her life's production.

Can you take on the lead role in your life?

- Say "I Love You," out loud to those you care for. Make it a habit to catch yourself feeling it, desiring to share it, and then verbalizing it.

- Talk to your oven and thank it for all of the fantastic meals it has helped you prepare.

- Watch a passionate couple in love and allow their energy to fill your well.

- Take the time to look at a stranger and smile.

- Tell the animals, plants, mountains, rain, and clouds how much you appreciate them.

- Recognize the love in the helping actions, positive attitudes, and kind gestures of others.

- Hug a neighbor, a spouse, a child, a friend. Everyone needs a hug.

- Kiss your arm enthusiastically and find out just how fun it is to truly love yourself. Why not?

Grandma lived a wonderful, love-filled life, and sharing that love with people and her environment came naturally to her. Yet, the greatest lesson I learned from Grandma was to love oneself.

Today, ask yourself: what *do* you love about you? Not the fluff stuff on the surface, but what are those difficult aspects of yourself that you have yet to embrace? What can you love about yourself today that you weren't willing to love yesterday?

- My aging skin

- My complicated style of thinking

- My difficulty in letting go of relationships

- My stretch marks

- My voice

- My aching body

- My ego

- My serious side

- My cellulite

- My pain over past mistakes and memories

If you can truly love yourself, then you are truly able to love others and the world around you. And that is the secret, isn't it?

I'm listening...

"Grandma" and "Love" were one and the same. While driving to meet a friend, it came to me. Rosa Moore... Rose-*Amor*. Rose and *Amor* ("love" in Italian) truly *were* indistinguishable!

Grandma Moore at 50

4

GETTING TO KNOW YOU

It was a sunny and gorgeous eighty degree fall day in September. Visiting Tucson in the summer months was not at the top of anyone's list of things to do since the temperatures hovered in the hundreds. As soon as the weather changed, though, Grandma and Grandpa would come to visit. I had just entered my sophomore year at Salpointe Catholic High School and was already busy with class assignments and after-school activities. I loved the beginning of the school year since it felt like an opportunity to start again in whatever arena I needed or wanted to change. New year. New opportunities. New choices.

One afternoon before a football game, I drove home with my best friend, Lynne, to get ready. Sitting outside on our brick patio was Grandma. We opened the sliding glass door and walked out. Grandma immediately sprang up from the black wrought iron patio chair where she had been reading and began her meeting-some-one-new ritual. "Getting to know you, getting to know all about you," she sang, as she strutted her way over to Lynne. She and I were still in our workout clothes from cheerleading practice, when I tried to prepare her for the infamous introduction with Grandma. "Getting to like you, getting to hope you like me," she continued as she cupped Lynne's face in her hands and gazed at her sweetly.

As her conversation-opener, Grandma sang this verse from one of her favorite musicals, *The King and I,* to each new person she met. The longer she carried the tune, the more time she took to hold your hand, rub your arm, and run her fingers through your hair. And as Lynne didn't back away or seem bothered, Grandma kept on singing.

"Haven't you noticed? Suddenly I'm bright and breezy. Because of all the beautiful and new, things I'm learning about you…" Her long, drawn-out syllables gave her more time to take in every detail on Lynne's face, memorizing each unique charac-teristic. A small dimple to the left of her mouth. A small scar above the eyebrow. Long sandy brown hair framing her oval-shaped face. Grandma looked intently at Lynne with a genuine desire to know more. Where did she get that smile? What accident created that scar? Does she resemble her father or her mother?

Lynne stood speechless. Coming from a family of stern parents and rough-and-tough older brothers, she always carried herself with a confident strength unlike any other girl I knew. She wasn't a warm and fuzzy kind of girl which intrigued me. Her aura of *feminine fierce* made me feel safe in her company. She tilted her head and looked over at me with a "Why is this lady singing to me?" gesture. Grandma's spontaneous approach came on so quickly, Lynne didn't have time to decide whether she liked it or not. No time to react thoughtfully. No time to rehearse a response. She had to speak honestly, or not at all.

"What is your name, dear?" Grandma asked as she held Lynne's arms and stood straight in front of her. Without leaving time for a response, Grandma continued, "You are so beautiful. My goodness."

"Lynne," she finally answered, as her nervous smile erupted into laughter. Without hesitation, Grandma reached out and pulled me in as well, now holding us both captive. That was Grandma. Breaking all of the illusionary teenage rules we thought we could control. So much for boundaries.

who am i?

Grandma knew that by asking questions and searching for answers, she was leading others to a deeper connection with themselves. For me, this action of "getting to know you" was more than a simple song expressing her interest in my life. Her tune carried me to a place of "Who am I?"—a place I constantly continue to visit.

It is common for many of us to go through life meeting others, yet avoiding taking the time to know ourselves. Sometimes we place ourselves last on the list of whom we know best. We allow others' expectations and personal fears to overshadow our true nature. We go through the motions of what we *think* others want to see, or say words we *think* others want to hear. We inevitably become so detached from the real sense of who we are that we are unable to express just that. So let's find out what moves us and inspires us and makes us sing!

putting your self into practice:

Day 1: Where are you spending most of your time?

Make a list of all the things you did today. This list may include:

Driving
Eating
Household chores
Working at your job
Talking on the phone
Exercising
Listening
Organizing
Writing
Playing
Sleeping
Watching television
Socializing

Once your list is made, write out the average amount of time spent on each area. Highlight any gaping holes or subjects that need a little more attention. Then note the areas that seem to take more time than you think is necessary. Bring steadiness into your day by staying aware of these highlighted sections, and then begin changing them to reflect a more balanced you.

Day 2: Who called or texted you today?

Make a list of each person who called, texted, or e-mailed you today. Carefully study the list. Is it work-related, or are friends or family members checking in? Does one friend call you three times a day or more? Do you find yourself repeating the same conversation with three different friends? Are these people enhancing your life? Are they draining your energy (or are you draining theirs)? How can you best serve others, while still serving yourself?

Look at the changes you can you make today to bring your communication into harmony with who you truly are.

Day 3: What did you eat today?

Make a list of every meal eaten. Notice any interesting facts about what you ate? Would you have eaten everything if you had paid attention to the taste? How does the food relate to how you are feeling? Is there any type of food that seems to be weighing you down, rather than lifting you up? Take the entire day to be aware of food.

Day 4: Where did you visit today?

Tune into the direction in which you are physically traveling. Did you go in a thoughtful, aligned manner? How is your physical way of traveling related to the emotional or intellectual space you are in? Do you feel as though you are on the right track, or were you backtracking, stuck in certain areas, or simply out of sync? When there is more than one way to get to your destination, try another route. If a voice inside says "turn right," even if you usually drive straight, turn right. Be open to insights or leads from your intuition. Be on the lookout for signs and beauty where you least expect them.

Day 5: How do you handle difficult issues in your life?

Begin to be aware of how you deal with life's challenges. Do you talk to as many friends as possible, or do you withdraw and spend the days in worry and anguish? Do you let your imagination run wild with various outcomes and stories that only add drama to the situation? Do you write your frustrations down on paper, let them sit a while, and then come back to them later? Do you ignore the challenge and hope it will go away? Or do you face the issue by looking at it head on and feeling the feelings?

Day 6: How did you express gratitude today?

When you first awoke, what thoughts filled your mind? Fill your day with more "thank yous" and notice how quickly your mood changes. Living in a state of gratitude generates kindness and consideration, not only for yourself but for all that exists around you. Be grateful, and grace will follow.

Day 7: Who are you today?

Today I am Interested in _____.

Curious about_____.

Happiest when_____.

Thankful for_____.

Hoping to_____.

Alive when_____.

Amazed at_____.

Open to_____.

Whatever you do, take note. Start paying attention to the processes and routines of your behaviors so you may begin to explore them. Are they effective and positive, or are they tiring and repetitive? Make checking in with yourself part of your daily meditation. "Who am I today?" Once you become more familiar with your essence, you can begin to fine-tune your power and self into the best spirit that reflects *you*.

I'm listening...

While on our recent trip to San Francisco, my husband Kelly and I strolled down the brick sidewalks of Chestnut Street, enjoying the sunny day. A stunning petite woman approached us, walking her Bichon.

Kelly looked at the dog, with its unmanageable locks and fur poofed out. "I love her haircut. What is her name?"

The owner smiled and sighed, "Oh, Coco is getting old and going blind, so I have to groom her myself."

Kelly asked her if she lived close by, adding, "Karen's Grandma Rosa lived here in the Marina."

"Oh, how fantastic. Yes, this is an incredible city to live in. I just love it here." She asked if we were considering moving.

"I would love to," said Kelly, "but I can't get Karen to move. She has a yoga studio in Tucson, where we live, and hasn't wanted to stop teaching."

The woman smiled and said, "Well, there are a lot of yoga studios right here on Chestnut." She pointed them out from where we were standing. She then said to me, "That explains why your energy is so calm." She looked straight into my eyes. "It is wonderful that you are so centered and focused. I'm with you, though. I understand why you don't want to move. My friends are here."

We spoke a few minutes longer, as I squatted down for Coco to give me kisses.

When they walked away, my entire body flushed with goose bumps. Directly above us hung a sign: *"Delarosa"*—of the rose. Again, divinely directed. A sincere, loving conversation while getting to know a woman who recognized me for who I am...courtesy of Grandma.

5

OUR FIRST SIGNS

It had only been three weeks since Grandma Rosa had passed, and I was still walking around with that sensitive opening at my heart's core. I had that feeling of existing in this world but truly feeling as though my soul was somewhere else. On that morning, Celina, our kind housekeeper, and I stood in the kitchen, reminiscing about the times when Grandma lived with us in our home.

Eight feet away, our television sat on the kitchen counter. Midsentence, the TV turned on. No remote, no buttons pushed, no explanation. It merely turned on. "Ooh, ooh!" Celina exclaimed. She shivered and opened her eyes wide. I stared at her; she stared at me. Our eyes veered toward the screen then back to each other.

I walked over, pressed the power button, and turned the TV off. We weren't sure what to think, dismissing it as odd for the moment. As we started up our conversation, it happened again. This time Celina grabbed my arms and clung to me. Chills ran down both of us. "It's Grandma." I said. "It's Grandma." We shook and shuddered while holding one another, our heartbeats racing as we stood, frozen.

The moment the kids walked in from school, I told them all about the unbelievable event. "Well, we weren't going to tell you, because we thought it was crazy," said Kim, my oldest daughter, "but yesterday, Christopher and I were sitting on the stools right here, and the stool closest to the TV moved and leaned itself sideways on the wall."

"Yeah, Mom. I saw it, too! We both thought it was so strange, we weren't going to say anything," my son Chris added, in his confident voice. At ages eighteen and fourteen, respectively, I knew that they weren't simply fabricating images.

I was thrilled. These bizarre happenings didn't take place every day. Kristina and Courtney, my other two daughters, were just as intrigued and amazed. Immediately, I called Mom and shared the astonishing events. Well, this just about sent Mom over the moon. In anticipation of another "sighting," she decided to come by the next day. All of us now buzzed about how, of course, Grandma showed up in the kitchen, her favorite room in the house. "Mom, I want to see a sign," said my mom, feeling left out. We laughed. Within minutes, from the other side of the kitchen. "Crrrrraaash!" A large ceramic tray fell out of its cabinet and onto the floor. How could that possibly happen? Sure, the cabinet door was open, but the trays were securely stacked inside each other.

The kids jumped up and ran around the kitchen, making ghost-like sounds after the obvious sign. How ironic that each time, at least two of us were present to witness these happenings. Not just one person, but at least two people seeing and hearing the same thing. "All right, Mom," said my mom. "We got it. We know you're here. You don't have to break any more dishes."

first step: denial

The beginning step to an open mind is denial, that automatic response of "not true," which we have when we hear something for the very first time. When we deny an unfamiliar idea, our mind and body react instantaneously. The initial bodily reaction may be a physical crossing of the arms—a blocking off of the new and unheard-of energy, which feels like an improbable or bizarre notion. It then moves into the thought, "I refuse to believe that," or "That can't be true."

Denial may not seem like a step at all. But when we hear suggestions or opinions that differ from our own reality, we are really just responding to a basic fear—fear of the unknown. Fortunately for us, this is a good sign.

With denial, our first response is "No." Our second response is still "No," but not as strongly felt. When we hear something for the third time, our response may be, "You know, I have heard that before. I am not sure if I believe it, but I have heard others speaking about it." Soon the idea is not so far-fetched. What once resided outside our comfort zone is now in our present realm of vision.

When we pause after a sensation of denial, we can ask ourselves the question, "What if this is true?" Maybe it is. Maybe it isn't. Believe or don't believe; that's not the point. The point is that either way, the *idea* does exist. It just comes down to whether or not we choose to allow the idea into our belief systems.

"Angels exist" is one example of a belief. The existence of angels may or may not be true. It may also be true, whether we believe it or not. We don't have to believe in anything we don't wish to believe in. But if we simply entertain the *idea* of angels existing, then we can think bigger and be open to more possibilities.

I never shied away from the idea of Grandma Moore connecting with me. When she died, I felt sorrowful and still hurting with the loss of her physical presence. But I wasn't mournful because I knew that her body of ninety years had given her an exuberant life. I always believed that I would continue to have a relationship with her. And I was right. Grandma Rose didn't waste any time setting up this new form of communication with us. She wanted to let everyone know right away, in as theatrical an approach as possible, that yes, she's still here.

Because Grandma was so outspoken on earth, I assumed she'd be a great communicator from the other side. I missed her words of encouragement, her "Bravos," but I could still hear them in my meditations and dreams. Any time I wanted to "be with Grandma," all I had to do was close my eyes and imagine her with me. I immediately pictured her swaying from side to side, singing and chatting.

What I hadn't foreseen was just how creatively Grandma would choose to connect—and I am glad that I didn't. Instead, not knowing has been a constant source of fun and wonder. I am always aware of the possibility of her presence in every situation. That alone has kept our relationship alive.

For thirty-six years, she played a hugely inspirational role in my life. Her support, guidance, and love carried me through then and still does now. To commemorate the corner in the kitchen where the TV turned on, the stool moved, and where Mom was standing, I hung a white cross with the lyrics of "Just In Time" scrolled down the front. I painted the cross especially with Grandma in mind. In the center, I placed one simple red rose, symbolizing her name and her continual presence here.

This cross was the first *it* cross I ever made. It was the first time I ever knew without a doubt, that *it* was exactly as it was meant to be. Once completed, I stated out loud, "This is it!" and *it* was the first of many.

What concepts immediately cause you to react with a "No" response?

What ideas, which you once thought foolish, do you now respect?

Which past beliefs assisted you during a certain phase of your life and then dissipated when new and more genuine ones came along?

Has anyone who has passed shown up in your life in unexpected ways?

How can you creatively commemorate loved ones and honor those who have passed?

I'm listening...

My daughter, Kristina, called me and said she wanted to bring something over. "I was looking through this magazine and saw an ad for a new fragrance by Oscar de la Renta. It's spelled R-O-S-A-M-O-R!" The excitement in her voice was palpable.

"C'mon, really?" I answered. I imagined Grandma sitting in on the meeting from the other side. "What shall we name our new perfume?" they vacillated. I pictured Grandma leaning down behind them, hinting persuasively clearly, *Rosa Moore. Rosa Moore.*" Why not? And of course, it was created by an Italian designer.

Part 2

HER LEADING MAN

GRANDPA–

The Palace of Fine Arts was a constant
amid change, as was my grandfather.

While sitting on his bench, reading and people-watching,

he calmly sat, smiled, and listened.

Inevitably one out-of-towner would ask him,

"Where is a good restaurant around here?"

"That's easy," Grandpa would answer. "Casa Rosa."

His love of my grandma's cooking was legendary.

Her Italian recipes kept him full and content,
and his tummy smiled because of it.

The visitor would then follow with,
"Where is this great restaurant?"

Grandpa would invite him over on the spot.

Although generally considered improper
behavior, Grandma Rosa loved it.

She loved her reputation for her
delicious meals and open door.

Sharing their love of their city with
others brought them pleasure.

6

GRANDPA MOORE: THE PEACEFUL ONE

My grandfather was the most peaceful, contented person I have ever known. Walter Frederick Moore was his full name, but Grandma called him Wally. I always thought that was a funny name—Wally.

Grandpa Moore looked like a genuine grandpa. He wore casual trousers with a tucked-in, long-sleeved shirt, leather belt, and comfortable walking shoes. His suntanned skin was filled with wrinkles from happy eyes and smiling cheeks. His square-shaped face, broad shoulders, and strong jawline gave him his rugged strong appearance. Eyeglasses, a watch, a pipe, his wedding ring, and a baseball cap were his only everyday accessories.

On his daily walks around the marina and Chrissy Field, he enjoyed chatting with retired neighborhood buddies and friendly boat owners. Generally, though, he walked alone slowly, with his hands clasped behind his back, always keeping his eyes on the ground in front of him. Frequently, he came home with surprises he'd found. While I was growing up, in every phone conversation, I asked, "Grandpa, did you find anything today?"

He always had some new treasure story of how a shiny silver coin in the grass caught his eye, or how a blown-away scarf had made its way to the rocky shore. In his front closet was an extensive collection of found hats, sunglasses, scarves, mittens, coins, and trinkets—all of which were passed on to whoever needed them.

"Hey, kiddo!" he would say. Even the sound of his voice was pure grandpa-like. His inflection and cadence sounded like a baseball announcer giving play-by-play highlights in the bottom of the ninth inning. After a patting-the-back hug, he would smile and ask, "How are you, dearie?" Not that he was going to offer any response to my answer of "just fine" or "pretty good." He only asked, listened, grinned, and cheered me on.

It's funny how I can't remember any truly significant conversation we had. What I do remember are his actions of a one-two elbow into my side and a double tilt with his head. It was like there was always a silent witty joke taking place—which only he was aware of. His quiet, rasping voice made our chats that much more intimate. Not once did he judge, critique, or tell me which direction to take. All he did was love, accept, and let me be. His winks and nudges always made me feel relaxed and at ease.

Grandma Rosa walked fast, spoke out, and was constantly changing. Grandpa, on the other hand, was quiet, simple, and settled. It was a balance that worked.

He was very creative in his methods of keeping the peace. In his later years, Mom often said, "Daddy, we need to get your hearing aid working, so you can hear us." As this subject was brought up often, he always replied, "Works fine, dearie," as he winked, making repetitive snickering sounds. He loved his silent space, and that included not having to listen to Grandma talk all the time. We understood and laughed. Maybe now I know the real truth— why our conversations were so simple and limited. He probably couldn't hear me.

everything is divine

My friend Cyndi came over to visit me after my hysterectomy, and as I showed her around, I pointed out a large, panoramic photograph of Grandpa, sitting on his bench at the Palace. She sighed at the photo with a smile and said, "I remember the day he died."

"Really?" I responded. It had been so long since his death; I had somehow forgotten the details of that day.

"I came over to paint," she said. "You were still in bed." It all started coming back to me. I had chosen to stay in bed, curled up in my cocoonlike shell, enveloped by that quiet, profound love that wraps us up when an adored grandparent dies.

Years ago, on the actual day of his passing, she had recommended we read *Angel Wisdom* for the day's message. Cyndi and I had shared many deep, moving conversations about our husbands, children, dreams, and philosophies. This book of daily meditations had always offered a centered, tangible focus for us as our faith and spirituality matured.

"It was the day of the Prayer of St. Francis," she recalled, as she gazed at Grandpa's photograph. "Remember? I'll never forget that."

I had forgotten! It had been fourteen years since my grandfather's passing, and although I was easily pulling images and memories about Grandma Rosa, I hadn't fully given much time or attention to Grandpa. Yet, a friend had been so touched by the moment and its genuine essence that she had recalled it freshly.

We visited for a bit longer, and after she left, I went downstairs to my bookcase and pulled out the heavily worn, stained paperback from the shelf:

September 27

Instrument of Peace

Lord, make me an instrument of Thy peace—
Where there is hatred, may I bring love;
Where there is wrong, may I bring the Spirit of
forgiveness;
That where there is discord, may I bring harmony;
Where there is error, may I bring truth;
Where there is doubt, may I bring faith;
Where there is despair, may I bring hope;
Where there are shadows, may I bring light;
Where there is sadness, may I bring joy;

Lord, grant that may I seek rather to comfort than to be
comforted;
To understand, than to be understood;
To Love, than to be Loved;
For it is by self-forgetting that one finds;
It is by forgiving that one is forgiven;
It is by dying that one awakens to Eternal Life.

Angel Wisdom, Taylor and Crain

The question posed on the page asked, "Are you willing to be the angel's instrument of peace? Next time you feel a lack of direction, meditate on this prayer and ask the angels for guidance, and soon you will know what to do."

I needed direction that day, as I had been healing from my surgery, and for weeks the anesthesia had clouded my thinking. Here, simply from a friend's visit, came exactly what I needed for my writing as well as my recuperation.

For a while, I thought that to write, I would have to put my life as I knew it on hold. I felt that it would be necessary to stop breakfast outings and teaching yoga classes. I even believed that chores would have to be hired out and meals made by others. All of those daily rituals and enjoyments would have to wait for a future time. I always imagined a writer writing in complete silence, locked away in some corner of the home, until the completion of that day's assignment had been met and the dark night had settled in. Now I know that those same activities I was ready and willing to postpone are the exact sources that stimulate ideas and feelings necessary for the brilliance of the pages.

This reaffirmed my belief that *life* is what fuels the fire. Time spent with friends, sharing in conversations, eating out at new restaurants, and practicing any form of exercise simultaneously mold the creative project at hand. So does having my kids over with their dogs for a swim party, or watching a great documentary with my husband, or having tea with a like-minded girlfriend. These are the life moments that are never meant to be replaced by something "better."

Have you ever considered working something you love to do into your day without waiting for the "right time" to do so? Do you wait until later to play tennis, take that cooking class, or learn a new language? Are you ready to turn that hobby into a career?

The time is now.

Place those activities at the top of your list, and see how joyful life is and can be. I came to play. What about you?

when grandpa died

The fact that I was not present with Grandpa Moore when he passed had always bothered me. Sadly, my mom told me not to come to the hospital when he was ill. "I don't want you to see him this way," she said. Although I now recognize her anxiety and hesitancy, I never understood the desire to exclude family members who wanted to be with their loved ones at such a significant moment.

At the time, I wanted to fly to San Francisco, and although I was told "Don't come," I wish I had. Sitting at home, I felt left out. I felt strong enough to have handled my grandfather's transition. Yet, why was I not strong enough to go against my mother's wishes?

I told her later that when Grandma or anyone else passed, I was going to be there. I did not want to miss those blessed moments again. There is a great power of love in the midst of death and dying, and my presence was not only important but strongly desired by my soul. This proved true with Grandma.

After my friend's recent visit, I decided to ask Mom about the day's details. She told me that she and her sister Barbara were at home with Grandma when they received the phone call from hospice early that morning. Grandpa had died in his sleep.

All of that time, all of those years, I had presumed that the family, including Grandma, was there by his side. But no! No grand exit. No big production. His choice was to leave quietly, just as it was his style to live quietly.

This shocked me, of course, but at the same time revealed the fact that all things are divine. Even if I had traveled to San Francisco to be with him, he would have chosen to pass without any of us there. Sometimes we believe we know what is best, when truly we have no control over what is divine.

I'm listening...

While on our recent trip to Calistoga and San Francisco, Kelly and I went to church. The priest announced that the next Sunday, they would celebrate the blessing of the animals with the Prayer of St Francis. Immediately, I thought of Grandpa Moore and knew he was softly making himself known. I recalled the meditation from *Angel Wisdom* and wondered if they always celebrated St. Francis on September 27th, the anniversary of his death.

Grandma Rosa; my brother, Fred; my
sister, JoAnn; Grandpa Moore; and me.

7

OPPOSITES

I knew well the opposite type of grandpa. While growing up with the quiet love of Grandpa Moore, I simultaneously experienced a grandfather who enforced the "do not speak unless spoken to" rule for us children. Grandpa Fred, my father's father, would, without hesitation, discipline us for speaking out of turn or for other misbehaviors. Deep, sharp, and authoritative, his voice could cut through the upbeat energy in a room at a moment's notice. I still have the clear image of him taking one of us, thankfully not me, over his knee for a full, flat-handed spanking in front of everyone. It set the tone for every future get-together.

As a young child, I feared our visits to see him. "Now, go give Grandpa Fred a hug and a kiss," my father would prod me. Here was a man whose energy threatened and scared me, and now I was supposed to give him a hug and kiss and pretend that everything was fine. Every time I saw him, anxiety, trepidation, and nausea filled my stomach. I never knew what his reaction would be or what misstep I would make to cause his angry outbursts.

At almost every big family holiday, he sat in his chair, while my siblings, my cousins, and I sat motionless on the floor in front of him, scolded for playing in the house or making too much noise. He took off his leather belt, folded it in half, and, holding both sides, *snapped* it loudly in front of us.

The atmosphere changed from chatty family celebration to one where you could hear a pin drop. Smiles disappeared. Eyebrows rose. Everybody stopped and watched. Nobody did anything. A jolt of fear sent waves through my system, traveling from my stomach up through my heart. These feelings quelled me. It took years for me to rescue and remove them.

Having polar opposites for grandfathers was confusing and illogical to me as a child. How could one grandfather be so openly affectionate, kind, and accepting, while the other was so firm, domineering, and strict? I was still the same me.

Of course, now with more understanding and maturity, I realize that people's environment, their ability to tolerate the rumpus and high energy of children, and their social and cultural upbringing all play into their actions and behaviors. With so many children in such a small space, I am sure his patience and tolerance levels were challenged.

But as a kid, I just wanted love.

"Your Grandma Josephine was a saint." Everyone I met told me so. She spent her days calmly making sure that each of her seven children and many more grandchildren were catered to, cared for, and looked after. Her gentleness and kindness shone through into every aspect of her life. Grandma Josephine passed away when I was young, and Grandpa Fred had the good fortune to marry and survive his second wife, Eva. He then spent his last happy years with my third grandma, Grandma Jere. Obviously, I have been blessed in the grandma department.

Grandpa Fred became a softie after he retired, and in his later years, we shared many very pleasant afternoons together. Two weeks after the birth of my first daughter, Grandpa Fred and Grandma Eva came for dinner at our apartment. I hadn't timed the meal well, and the chicken I prepared came out of the oven completely shrunken, overcooked, and literally black. He assured me, "It tastes just fine," as he smiled and ate every tough bite. At that moment my entire perspective changed. His compassion for me, as a new mother and wife, melted my heart and made me weep.

After he died, I sat in meditation, feeling his presence. I sensed his sadness for his earlier behavior. He knew I was scared of him when I was little. "I'm so sorry." I imagined his genuine apology floating into my mind. I then sensed him sending his love to everyone and heard the words, "There is always hope." Facing fears was a difficult yet wonderful lesson to learn, and I thanked him for taking on such an important role in my life.

go to your room

When I was growing up, my father always said, "If you can't be happy, then go to your room." Showing emotions that were less than jovial was not handled well in the family space. So I spent many days and nights and hours in my room by myself, thinking, imagining, and crying. Those lonely moments swarmed through my body, sinking into my soul's center.

I was internally anguished or, more likely, perplexed during my childhood. I always knew my parents loved my brother, my sister, and me. They took excellent care of our needs and always gave us opportunities to learn and explore. We grew up in a spacious home on an eighteenth fairway and attended private Catholic schools. My parents would save up all year to take us on adventurous motor home trips throughout the United States, as well as vacations to Hawaii and Europe.

Fair, generous, driven, and hardworking, my dad succeeded at business, appreciated a good joke, and thrived on being health conscious. He accumulated boxes of awards and memorabilia from his earlier years as a prominent disc jockey, popular comedian, and media brokerage owner. *The Prophet,* by Khalil Gibran, sat forever on his bedside table—a book I confiscated and adored at a very early age. We drove places together, listening to cassette tapes of *Erroneous Zones* by Wayne Dyer, while looking for *and finding* the closest parking spots. A perpetual teacher, Dad had a powerful influence on my life, time and time again, without even knowing it.

My mother, Judi, had a Jacqueline Kennedy Onassis look and style about her. Classy, artistic, and organized, her ability to look great in cutoffs and to stretch one meal to feed many proved inspiring. Her calm ability to adapt in any situation astounded me. She fell into a category I created—"reflectionate." Reflective and affectionate. She always mirrored the energy and attitude of whomever she was with, exhibiting a deep compassion for their feelings. Gentle and lighthearted, she had an ease about life and all that came with it.

From my very young perspective, I marveled at my parents' lives. I wanted to be just like both of them. Early on, a personal pledge to "make them proud" ensued.

With all of the choices they offered, it was obvious that my parents loved us. Yet, never hearing the actual words left me puzzled. Having to say, "Yes, sir" and "No, sir," or "Yes, ma'am" and "No, ma'am" to my own parents seemed so foreign to my innate concept of love. It signified respect, yes, but it always kept my hopes of closeness an arm's length away. So my room saw a lot of me.

And simply walking into my room didn't mean that the feelings of sadness stopped. I just felt them alone, rather than with my family. As time passed and the stresses of being me grew, I was unable to understand all of my increasing emotions by myself; I really didn't know how to handle them. Admittedly, I didn't handle them well. I stuffed them down into my stomach, where I layered them one on top of the other. Anger, unhappiness, confusion, disregard, doubt, fear, disappointment…On the outside, my mission in life turned into being "the good girl" and "the one who's so involved," in order to gain attention and keep the peace within my family.

And I had every reason to be happy. I had a family. I had a home. I had my own room. I had clothes and toys and a bed all to myself. So what was wrong with me? Why, at times, was I so miserable? My irrational laundry list of reasons probably looked similar to that of others. *I am not loved. Nobody really cares about me. I don't fit into my own family.*

Whatever the case, the feelings *felt* real. I didn't have the tools necessary to deal with my sensitive, changing self. And the fact that I didn't have anyone to talk things over with, as the subject was deemed "negative," wasn't good. So the conversation was all in my head, and the feelings ran rampant inside me.

Throughout my childhood and teenage years, due to habit, I simply went to my room as soon as I came home. My time there seesawed between two opposite worlds—depressed and alone, yet also delighted, imaginative, and peaceful. I spent some of my most inventive and creative moments there, where the silence gave my good thoughts room to expand, strengthen, and grow. Ideas and discoveries came to me repeatedly. My room became a place where stuffed animals turned into best friends, cardboard boxes transformed into robots, and ink and paper rested together as poetic phrases.

And now, at this very second, I am once again in my room. It, too, has been a refuge of two worlds. It is the room where Kelly and I have sat as we spoke honestly about our marital challenges. And the same space where we confronted our son about his drug use. This room has been witness to many real events and has offered itself as a safe haven for the truth. I have prayed and meditated in each inch of air here, and my gratitude tangibly lingers. My room is a place where words become works and dreams become realities. It is a special sacred space that exudes its healing power over me and all who enter. I am so happy that I have had the chance to "go to my room."

I'm listening...

My much-loved friend, Tina Powers, possesses the healing gift of tuning in to people who have passed on. Weeks after Grandma's death, when Tina first began to trust her insights, Grandma Rosa made herself known. Her presence was bold and up-front, with no lack for words to share. "*Ciao, bella,*" Tina said, as she heard rapid-fire kisses coming at her. Grandma shared insights worth pondering. "If you can uncover more of the places that are dark, the more brilliant your light will shine." Her inspiring words continued, "Don't ever worry. The less you worry, the more room you have for love." With goose bumps and tears, I listened to the conversation for hours.

Patiently content in the background, Grandpa Moore appeared, with his calm, gentle energy. Tina softened her smile and tilted her head with a sweet "Ahhh..." at the feeling of him. She said that one of his jobs on the other side was to greet people who have recently passed. Can you think of a better person for such a position? I can just imagine him saying, "Hello, dearie," with his one-two elbow. "How's it goin'?" And then he would simply be with them and listen, like he always did with me.

Part 3

SAN FRANCISCO CHARM

SIMPATICO–

From my eyes as a child, I saw the similarities.

Grandma Rosa and San Francisco—

Lending desirable destinations,

Displaying unique personalities,

Offering stimulating paths,

Delivering great food.

And when both exist in the same setting,

The two eventually become one.

Grandma Rosa and San Francisco—

A duet made in heaven.

8

2200 BEACH STREET

Traveling alone for the first time at age eleven, I was greeted with layers of hugs and kisses at the airport by my grandparents. After a conversation-filled drive home along the bay, we arrived at their infamous 2200 Beach Street apartment in San Francisco. I had inked this address many times from my letter writing; and now, peering through the scrolling metal gate to the foyer, was like waiting outside Willy Wonka's Chocolate Factory. I held the iron bars and couldn't wait to see what was inside.

Grandpa unlocked the gate for Grandma and me to enter. The lobby looked like it was straight out of the movies, with its granite floors, wallpapered walls, and pressed tin ceiling. Once in, I raced up the three flights of stairs to the top floor. "You have to go up and down these stairs every time you go out?" I yelled back over my shoulder, panting heavily. "Whew!"

Grandma glided right past me. While I was catching my breath, Grandpa opened the door and set his keys down. I stepped onto the creaky wooden floor and took it all in. A mirror hung on the wall directly across the entry area of their one-bedroom apartment. Below it sat a small two-shelved bookcase filled with vintage books.

"Now, let me show you around," Grandma said. Grandpa took my luggage to the other room as Grandma held me by her side and guided me in. "This is my precious *Great Books Collection*, which I purchased some years ago. They are my pride and joy." The hardbound, happily worn bindings with color-coded covers included works by Faust, Dante, and Chaucer.

She introduced us. "Ahhh, *Don Quixote*," Grandma said, as though he were a personal friend. She pulled out her favorites and held them up to her chest, reverently embracing them. Her appreciation of literature was absolutely alive. "And Shakespeare's *Romeo and Juliet*," she added. Her delicate fingers gracefully swept through the air as she motioned across the shelves. She leaned down, whispering, as if others could hear her, "These are going to be yours someday."

In the living room, the tour continued. She presented each piece of furniture, with its short history and special qualities. There sat the side table given to my grandparents by a neighbor and friend, John Adams. "He was a direct descendant of President Adams. Such a dear and interesting man," she told me. "His wife passed away, and he has no children, so we became his family." This was a story Grandma loved to share often.

I looked around the living space and saw an antique rocker and a veined marble and iron table, which she humorously pretended to lift as she showed off its sturdy weight. "Ughhh." Then there was a gorgeous hand-blown purple vase from Italy. She gave all of the pieces their moments of fame. "If it's not paying rent, it's outta here." Grandma told me. She didn't have any desire for cleaning up clutter and spending unnecessary time dusting. Every piece was "put to work," she added. It had to have a useful purpose and bring her pleasure, if it was to be in her possession.

"These are my babies," she exclaimed, as she pointed to her oil paintings, including one of a young boy with dark hair and green eyes. She was rightfully proud of her painted landscapes, portraits, and still lifes. Each one showcased her artistic abilities. Not knowing much about art, I wasn't really sure what determined a great piece versus an ordinary one, but there was no doubt in Grandma's mind—her originals were the best.

I followed Grandma around the room, amazed, listening to the special details and utter warmth she held for her collections. She treated artwork, furniture, and literature with high regard and gratitude, similarly to how she treated people. Every object complemented every other object in its place. I don't recall a single item under her care that she didn't love.

Seeing her delight in her own home left a lasting impression on me. It seemed clear to me then that if we surround ourselves with what makes us happy, we will be happy. And Grandma obviously was. The irony was that although she enjoyed her items greatly, she also freely gave them away. As she grew older, she accepted the fact that her time was winding down, so anyone who expressed an equal love of one of her pieces left her home with it in his or her arms. A table, a lamp, a bowl...size didn't matter. Off it went with the new owner.

She also made her wishes clear about certain specific pieces she wanted to hand down to family and friends. Her painting of a young boy with brown hair and hazel eyes turned out to bear a strong resemblance to my son, Christopher. Grandma made sure that we were to be the keepers of this for him. It now hangs outside his bedroom. My library also hosts her most prized and pleasing collection, her fifty-seven volume set of *Great Books*. Chaucer, Dante, and Shakespeare are now in good company with Katie, Walsch, and Shinn. Thank you, Grandma. I *love* them.

if you love it, it will work

Just like Grandma, greeting people at my door and giving them "the tour" has always been my way of welcoming others comfortably into my home. Sharing my interesting art pieces, two of which were trunk-painted by an Asian elephant named Desi, and bringing new life into old spaces has been a progressive passion of mine. During my younger days of designing, Mom introduced me to Mona, a bubbly, artsy woman who was moving to San Miguel de Allende, Mexico, and who was in the process of selling all of her furniture and artwork. She exuded the same confidence, originality, and eclectic style that Grandma did. When I walked into her home, I was immediately inspired by her ability to mix French, country, Middle Eastern, and contemporary pieces casually, yet brilliantly.

I was particularly enamored by a beautiful acrylic painting in bright, bold colors, depicting an Italian countryside with tree-dotted hills with homes and gardens. This three-by-three-foot acrylic painting simply took my breath away. The cobalt blue sky popped with color as it framed the black-tiled roofs of the simple, yet striking cottages. I asked her how much it cost. She kindly and succinctly said, "Four." I stood back and savored the shades, focusing on its straightforward, yet masterfully imagined layout. Four hundred dollars was a lot of money for me to be spending on art at that time. Unable to make the big purchase, I left with a wanting but "waiting to see how I felt the next day" attitude. The following morning I promptly called Mona. "I would love to own it. I couldn't sleep all night because all I could envision was that painting." She laughed and said it was mine. I rushed over to her house with my checkbook and paid her the four hundred dollars. We hugged, and she smiled, knowing how much I loved her piece.

While decorating my new home, many times I would simply sit on the floor in the empty room and wait—wait for a sign, a vision, a feeling, or a voice to offer direction as to what that space desired. It took time and energy to sit patiently and to willingly receive guidance from something greater than a catalog or a showroom. Inspiration came from a pillow, a card, a vacation. Any small feeling that moved me was built upon for the final plan. The colorful canvas of the Italian countryside became the entire inspiration for my kitchen, the room that took me the longest to design. It completely set the tone, with its cheerful energy and bright hues. It is the heart of the space, and everything else reflects it.

On that first day, I asked Mona, "How did you bring all of your styles together?" She said, "If you love it, it will work." I hadn't fully looked at life from the perspective of what I loved. But now I ask myself, "Do I love it?" before every purchase, every decision, every invitation, every job opportunity, and every travel destination. "If I love it, it will work!" I have repeated those words often, as they truly have given me all the direction in design and in life that I needed. Every paint color, menu item, song selection…they all had a new category to fall into. If I love it, it will work. And so a new dimension begins.

I'm listening…

While at Mona's house after purchasing my bright hillside painting, I caught a glance of a six-foot-tall rooster, painted by the same artist, with the same bright, sharp colors that just made me glad. I asked Mona, "How much is *this* painting?" She replied, "Twelve." Well, that was definitely out of my budget, so I sadly declined.

I drove home with my newly acquired landscape and my heart singing. Yet, a few days later, I realized that I just couldn't stop thinking about that painting of the rooster. I had the countryside piece, which I loved, but I decided I would love the rooster as well, even if it did cost a lot. I called Mona and asked if she still had it for sale. She said, "No. I'm sorry. I sold it."

"Oh…" My heart sank. I softly muttered, "For how much?"

"Twelve thousand," she said.

I paused. Wait! Twelve *thousand* dollars?

The magnificent countryside painting I paid four hundred dollars for was meant to be four *thousand*? And she didn't say anything. She didn't ask me for more money. She didn't make a face. She didn't even flinch because she knew I loved her painting as much as she did. She wanted *me* to have it. So I do.

9
WORKS OF ART

During my first visit to San Francisco, Grandma and Grandpa took me for a walk around the Marina neighborhood where they lived. I felt like a celebrity visitor. Every friend, neighbor, store clerk, trash collector, gardener, and mailperson had heard stories about me and where I was from. "Your grandparents talk about you all the time," they told me.

We walked down the sidewalk, noticing all of the flower planters, window treatments, and hanging chandeliers. Just a block away, Grandpa pointed out the bay window of the home where Joe DiMaggio lived. "Every time I see him out front, I say, 'Hey, Joe, How's it goin'?'" as he snickered with his usual leaning-in elbow to my side. "Joe's a nice guy and always waves and says, 'Good to see you.'"

From every angle, I saw beauty. The facades, the Palace, the people. Grandma planned my entire visit around what she thought I would love to do. It was a remarkable sensation, to be so bombarded with such loving attention. I felt more than important. I felt cherished.

Grandpa sat on his bench reading his book while Grandma and I made our way to the Exploratorium for the day. Grandma assured me that she was quite happy just sitting and people watching, while I delved into the museum's exhibits. She never rushed or hurried me; rather, she encouraged me to play, to be curious, and to take advantage of all the different experiments and displays. I twirled spinning spheres that resembled Earth and the planets and heard clear messages from another kid across the room while standing under an acoustically designed, scooped-out wall. Just the fact that Grandma was so prepared to sit gave me a greater freedom to have fun.

All week we dashed from museums to parks, enjoyed movies and markets, and played games and cards. On Saturday, we packed up the car to go to Golden Gate Park for a picnic and concert. Walking through the crowd felt daunting; I had never been in a place with so many people. Blankets and chairs were laid out on every hill and under every tree, spreading out through the entire park. Dogs on leashes, children throwing balls…everywhere I turned, families and friends played, relaxed, and awaited the afternoon's performance with Arthur Fiedler and the San Francisco Pops Orchestra.

The three of us made our way through the deep crowd until we came to a place far beyond the band shell. It was a lovely, sunny day as we laid down our blanket on the ground and settled in.

We unwrapped our Italian sub sandwiches, which I had helped Grandma make earlier that morning, and lounged back in the grass.

The Pops' triumphant marches and soft overtures filled the air. Clear, crisp notes hung above us with each melody, as the music flowed across the park. Grandma and I swayed together to the "Sound of Music Medley" and kicked our feet in the air during the "Cabaret" sequence. Grandpa grinned and bobbed his head when "Syncopated Clock" played and sat up tall with his shoulders back, marching to "Pomp and Circumstance." Dazzling and victorious, each piece inspired a different vivid picture in my mind.

Just before the program ended, we gathered our things and strolled through the park, away from the mass of people. Out of nowhere, we happened upon a cluster of tables covered with bins full of wood scraps and bottles of glue. Looking over, I could see mesmerized kids, standing and carefully pasting odds and ends together. Anyone interested in creating wooden sculptures for a small fee could do so. Grandma asked, "Would you like to, Karen?" I did.

I wandered through the maze of tables into the scrap wood designing zone. Instantly ideas popped into my mind. The possibilities were endless. A triangle on top of a rectangle, next to an odd angular piece. Geometric shapes of all kinds with bits of two-by-fours filled the boxes below. I built and glued and added layers to my rising formations. In an imaginative trance, I could have stayed all day.

The sun had been extra warm, and Grandpa, who had been good-naturedly waiting on a bench with Grandma, decided it was time to go. I gathered my three new formations, and we each carried one back to our car. Home at the apartment, my "works of art" were given prime property on the living room coffee table. Intently, we looked at the angles and designs of my intergalactic spaceship; my sky-flying sailboat; and my multilevel, high-tech, architecturally awesome office building, noting their originality.

"Wow," said Grandma, as I described my masterpieces. This experience gave me far more than the simple opportunity of gluing wooden parts together; it opened up an entirely new world of imagination I had never played in before.

After all of our excited conversation about the music, the park, and the sculptures, we put on our pajamas and got ready for bed. Following such a rewarding day, I stayed awake, smiling, all night. There was nothing quite like the feeling of being so free to build and invent, without any guidelines or rules.

When it came time for me to travel home, Grandma said, "Let's wrap them up gently." We carefully packed my suitcase with the spaceship nestled between my clothes, so I could still have a free hand to carry my two other creations. I hadn't thought out the "travel home part" when constructing my heavy boat or when stacking my tall building, which stood a good foot or so high.

I'm listening...

After the tragic San Francisco earthquake of '89, Grandma showed me saved pieces of broken gold-rimmed china she had found on the sidewalk in front of Joe's house. She pointed out their delicate details and expensive markings, noting that they *must* have belonged to Marilyn.

Once home, I carefully placed them on a shelf in my room. They never looked like much to the outsider, but what I saw was emotional freedom. For years, I gazed at the memories that traced back to my one incredible day of creating my "works of art" at the park.

the kids' painting

"When are we going to paint this, Mom?" The kids asked me this question almost every day. For two full years, a custom-made, twelve-foot-by-five-foot prepared canvas leaned up against our long living room wall. After moving into our spacious empty home, a friend had suggested that my kids paint their own piece for the room which was so overwhelmingly large. Having the huge canvas constructed was one thing, but getting up the courage and "oomph" to paint it was another.

Its enormity was beyond intimidating. Doubts ran through my mind every day as I faced the monstrous canvas. "I don't know where to begin. I don't want to make a mistake. What if it doesn't turn out?" Finally, I decided it was time to stop talking about it and just do it. I bought the kids white clothes, got out the colored paints, and set the date.

Before starting, I asked Kimberly, Kristina, Christopher, and Courtney to sit down and write out ten things that made them happy. A quick list: rainbows, eating artichokes, long showers… Then I had them write out ten things they *loved* to do: ride bicycles, swim, play games…Their enthusiasm grew as they wrote.

We grabbed the paints, ladder, buckets, and stirring sticks and walked down to an open dirt area outside, where I had already set up the canvas. Each of them chose his or her favorite color and then, one by one, stood at the top of the tall ladder. "Make a happy wish," I said. "Then toss up the paint."

Eagerly, they each flung the cup of paint up into the air and watched and shouted as it fell to the canvas below. Kim, the oldest, started it off with her favorite color, red. Her voice pitched with the paint as it flew. Kristina, with the color purple, let out a big shout: "Whooooo!" Excitement and anticipation grew with each turn. It was no surprise when Christopher chose teal, for it had been his favorite color all nine years of his young life.

Courtney climbed up the ladder. She had picked pink, of course. Everything in Courtney's five-year-old life was pink—her Barbies, her clothes, her hair bows, her bedding. She loved pink. With a bucket full of her favorite colored liquid, she threw her arms up in the air. The paint went up and then went down—on top of her *and* the ladder! Her shoes were coated in pink as well as each lower step. The kids and I cheered and doubled up laughing.

Every time they finished their turn, I walked over to them and patted their backs with my paint-covered hand, saying, "Good job, good job." They soon caught on, congratulating each other as well. "Yeah, good job." Pat, pat. Before we knew it, we were covered with a full array of colorful handprints and finger marks. Once they got into the rhythm of it, the piece effortlessly came together. I walked around with a paintbrush, adding splatters to a few open areas. Shapes fashioned in front of us—a horse, an octopus, and ladies' legs. Together we played as artists.

We carried all of our supplies and buckets back up to the house. Our massive canvas sat outside, drying in the front, leaning against two pillars. I asked the kids to pose, and "Ta Da!" Our Christmas card photo for that year was done as well. The following week, Courtney's friend commented on the amazing painting and asked how long it had taken to paint. Courtney, in her calm, factual voice, replied, "Two years." *She was right!* One day to paint, but two years to decide.

I always wanted to hang the ladder on the wall next to the painting. It just seemed as though they belonged together.

I'm listening...

I opened a fortune cookie today. "Big things coming in future. Only matter of time." A ten-foot canvas finished after two years. The message was obviously true.

"defunking" the system

Have you ever felt frustrated or discouraged due to attempt after attempt at changing what seemed to be impossible to change? We make thousands of decisions each day. Or *do* we?

Many times the brain gets into a rigid response pattern, which can feel like being in a rut. We go about our day with the same mind-set, the same routines, and the same outcomes. And then we wonder why we can't change. So often we try by changing our thoughts about a certain behavior, or *thinking* we should change them. And we go at it full force, deciding, "I am going to stop smoking cigarettes," or "I am not going to call my friend every time I need to vent," or "I am going to lose ten pounds."

These attempts may work for a short while. But we undoubtedly find ourselves back into our habitual ways of dealing with things because we just don't know how else to handle them. This desire to change something without success can leave us feeling helpless and out of control.

When behaviors such as gossiping, complaining, excusing, arguing, and such have been in place for days, weeks, months, and years, the ability to change that behavior becomes increasingly difficult. As time goes on, the behavior's momentum builds, like wheels spinning in deeply carved-out tracks. The brain falls into a groove; it does what it has been told to do for so long that it runs on autopilot and no longer looks for leads from us.

This is the best time to "defunk" the system—a concept I created, meaning to undo, unclog, and unblock our mind, allowing our intuition, compassion, and joy to flow through and take their natural places. Creating a quiet space between thoughts makes room for great insights, brilliant ideas, glimpses of future events, and messages from passed loved ones. It takes the "me" out of the equation, which makes life much more interesting.

In the beginning, we should not trust our minds. It has been misled by the subconscious into believing that its "story" is true. No story is true. The thoughts themselves receive way too much of our attention. Just because I have a thought doesn't mean it's important, real, or even necessary to follow. Some thoughts are just thoughts, nothing more.

When defunking the system, we challenge our minds to think differently and shock the system from running its patterned course. Through this coming-in-the-back-door method, we surprise the brain, making it stop to readjust, which then allows us a momentary opportunity to guide and direct our own thoughts once again. It is in that space that we experience the mystical, the magical, and the miraculous.

The first step to take when defunking the mind is to stop the expected response to the thought:

> If my thought is to wear a blue shirt, I wear green.

> If I want to brush my hair, I brush my teeth.

If I want to sleep in, I get up.

If I want to drive to the bank first, I go to the market.

If I want to turn left, I turn right.

If I want to eat a salad, I eat a sandwich.

If I want to drink tea, I drink water.

If I want to work on the computer, I go for a walk.

If I want to exercise, I lie down.

If I want to lie down, I exercise.

If I want to talk on the phone, I stay in silence.

Anything *and everything* I can do to stop the automatic response of being directed by what my brain wants me to do, I do. Every thought has a reaction. We should challenge that reaction immediately, by changing our repeated reply, and continue to do so until the automation stops.

After this defunking takes place, we will become aware of an alteration in our minds. Instead of the habitual answer to every question that arises, our minds now sit silently, awaiting direction *from* us and our great intuition.

Soon, thoughts we choose to think, actions we choose to perform, and behaviors we choose to practice will occur. Our intuitive selves will be in control. Our minds will now be at our whim, rather than the other way around.

Try this out for yourself. See what happens when you challenge every detailed direction your mind sends you. Give yourself at least a week to notice a difference in your thought patterns, and then keep it going until you have a quiet nonresponse at every choice posed. Then listen. Choose. Be guided. You'll find that you can manifest your own destiny and be guided at the same time. Congratulations on getting back to *you*, and have fun defunking your system.

10
FEEDING THE PIGEONS

While writing this book, I came to a place where I couldn't recall another story or aspect of Grandma that I wanted to share. I couldn't think because of a loud rumbling noise above my office. So I took a break, made some tea, and went outside to watch the sunrise. As I sat there, again I heard the bumbling noises.

It was then when I looked up and realized that pigeons were cooing on the roof above me.

Pigeons! Of course. "Thank you, Grandma."

How could I leave out the pigeons?

Grandma always stocked up on stale bread before I came to visit, knowing that one of the first things on the list of things to do was feed the pigeons at the Palace. One block away from my grandparents' apartment stood the Palace of Fine Arts, a picturesque dome surrounded by tall colonnades with figures of ladies at the top and an out-of-a-fairy-tale enchanted lake, which reflected the entire setting once again. Willow trees swooned, giving shade to the grassy areas surrounding it.

Foreigners and locals alike ventured to this locale for idyllic photos and visits with the pigeons, ducks, and swans. On any given Saturday, as many as a dozen bridal couples would arrive with their bridal parties for wedding portraits under the majestic dome and pillars and around the shimmering lake.

Just outside Grandma's apartment, I would run ahead, find the perfect bench, sit down, and let the frenzy begin. All it took was the crinkling of the bag, and with a loud "whoosh," flocks of pigeons would land at my feet. Harmonies of cooing sounds and teams of bobbing heads surrounded me. Grandma and I always sought the spotted one with the missing leg or the smaller one off by himself. We tried even harder to reach the ones that were limping or had broken wings.

Many times the pigeons flew onto my arms and into my lap, until all I could feel were the fluttering of their feathers stroking me. One or two would inevitably become my favorites of the day because of their trust and comfort while in my hands. I communicated with them by sitting still and waiting. "Hi guys. Did you miss me? I missed you." I actually hoped that they had remembered me from the previous time and, in some small way, that they needed me. But now, looking back, I see that it was I who needed them.

People walking by took pictures, while my grandparents grinned with pleasure. We offered bread to any onlooker who was interested. "Here you go. Have a slice." Together we all shared in the bonding time with nature. I tore the bread into small pieces, so it would last as long as possible, until I eventually sprinkled the very last crumbs out of the bag. When the flurry was over, I just sat there, believing that they were better off because of me.

Pigeons—they bring out the best and the worst in people. Grins or grimaces, trust or fear, tolerances or frustrations. The truth is, when Grandma first took me on this adventure, I was a bit nervous. Literally, walking up, I felt anxious about touching birds and having them touch me. And how about the possibility of them pooping on my head! Grandma had obviously fed them many times before. After the first friendly soul perched upon me, I relaxed. I just hoped for the best and knew that any accident could be easily cleaned up back at home. Thinking back now, it is amazing how many simple lessons I learned from the act of feeding pigeons:

- Be patient, and you will earn trust.

- Treat all equally.

- Always take extra care of those who need it.

- Give and you shall receive.

- Do not waste.

- Do not be afraid.

- It's OK to have fun.

- Sharing feels good.

- Forget what seems logical, and do what feels natural.

Our feathered friends are truly winged messengers in more ways than we may know. They lend us the opportunity to draw upon the feelings of home and family and alert us to important messages from unexpected sources. Think about it—the most popular travel destinations and tourist spots always have pigeons present. San Marco Square—pigeons. The Eiffel Tower—pigeons. Central Park—pigeons.

The only occasion they visited my Tucson home was on that one day, when they cooed so loudly that I couldn't get my work done. Since then, doves have nested, falcons have hunted, hawks have hovered, and hummingbirds have slept. Yet, not once have the pigeons come back to my rooftop. Message delivered successfully.

Palace pigeons and me.

san francisco revisited

On my last visit to San Francisco, I fervently set out to the Marina district once again for a view of the Palace Lake and a walk around my grandparents' old neighborhood. Kelly and I joined a new friend, Alyssa, who had offered to take photographs of me while there. We arrived to find the Palace of Fine Arts even more captivating than I had remembered. Expensive renovations to the structures, the landscaping, the paths, and the lake over the past few years had made the area sparkle even more. I quietly gazed at the water, looked into the trees, and walked along the sidewalk until I saw them—pigeons.

"Oh, I can't believe it! Again, how could I have forgotten about the pigeons?" I told her. I walked over to the edge of the lake, surrounded by freshly planted snapdragons and poppies. Slowly, I sat down next to my feathered friends on the newly built rock wall. Memories flooded in. Cooing sounds, shimmering purples and greens in their feathers, one-footed and two, timid and strong. "They haven't changed," I said, smiling.

I wished I had stopped to get bread from a market. All of a sudden, Kelly stepped up and handed me a crumbled cracker from our bag. "Yes. Let the festivities begin." Calmly, I waited for the first brave soul to come to me, as I held the crumbs in my hand. It always takes one to lead the crowd. Soon pigeons were on top of my hand, gazing into my eyes, and standing next to me. People rushed over and gathered with fascinated interest. Instantly, twenty Japanese tourists surrounded us, snapping pictures and asking us to pose with them. One woman, with multiple cameras and lenses around her neck, approached us with a smile. "Look," she said, as she held up her camera screen, showing a photo of me, beaming and holding a pigeon in my hand. Kelly laughed and handed her some of our snacks to help spread the joy.

The Palace still glimmered its magical light around the neighborhood. It felt so good, knowing that some things are still the same. The same enthusiasm shared by visitors, the same lagoon with swans and ducks, and the same beauty greater than words can explain. As the renovator for the Palace said, "And of course, it wouldn't be a city park without pigeons."

I'm listening...

On one visit Grandma proudly rushed me over to the Exploratorium for her surprise. "Come see! Come see!" There, above the entrance to the gift shop, hung a six-foot-wide panoramic photo. Caught on print were the Palace, the lake, the birds, and my grandfather, sitting on his bench, reading. There he was, captured in time, doing what he loved.

As a gift that next Christmas, Mom gave my brother, my sister, and me each a copy of the photograph. Mine now hangs in my bedroom, above my fireplace and directly across from my bed. The Palace, the lake, and Grandpa. It is so nice, waking up to a moment where beauty and love are captured together.

all in good time

How do you look at time? Do you let your watch determine your attitude, with a sense of rushing or waiting? How often do you find yourself feeling limited by time? The moments where we act and react due to thoughts of "There isn't enough time," or "If only I had more time," or "I am running out of time."

Some people seem to move effortlessly through their day, completing projects and enjoying their activities. They seem to "take their time" when it comes to getting things accomplished and take pleasure in the process "at the same time." Could it be that the constrictions of time have been released from their mental structure and, rather than arguing with what is, they seem to accept and enjoy and adapt to being just in time?

At any moment, we can go back and see and feel from new perspectives. Our past memories, which we have hung onto, suppressed, felt inhibited by, or disapproved of, can be transformed into new memories at this present time. What was difficult to accept "at the time" can now be reflected upon with compassion and mature knowledge. Difficult experiences can become brilliant gifts in time.

Do you hear words thrown around like, "I have time to kill," or "I'm just wasting time?"

Wouldn't it be more enjoyable to have "time to spend?" And isn't it wonderful when the universe allows an opening in the day for that unplanned "free time" to do whatever we please? In fact, we have nothing *but* time. We all have the same amount of time. It's what we choose to do with it and how we choose to spend it that matters. Honestly, we have so much to do—and so much time.

I'm listening...

So often this past year I heard the title song from *The Most Happy Fella* and thought of Grandpa Moore, enjoying his retired life in San Francisco. I hadn't listened to the actual words of the song until recently, after realizing that the song always came on when I was thinking about him. Wouldn't you know the subjects included an Italian gentleman falling in love with Rosabella in San Francisco.

11

BEAUTY NIGHT

"Come here, honey. Let's put your hair back and steam your face first," Grandma suggested. She wrapped my hair into a white towel and began filling the sink with hot water, beginning our evening beauty ritual. "Now, lean over the sink gently. Careful not to touch the water." She covered my head and the sink with a lightweight cloth and told me, "Slowly inhale and exhale for a few minutes, while the steam opens your pores and clears your head." It always felt a bit claustrophobic to me; I sounded like an astronaut on the moon, breathing in her helmet. Wanting to relax, it was easier for me to just close my eyes and notice the beads of sweat roll down my face into the sink. After a few minutes, I arose with a fresh gasp of air followed by the fresh water rinsing of my skin.

After a quick pat dry, I gently rubbed on Grandma's mixture of cornmeal and cleanser, exfoliating my chin, nose, and forehead. After a cool rinse, Grandma daubed my face lightly with soft, delicate touches of a towel, gently focusing on every inch of me. Smooth and soft, my skin felt brand new.

"Now we're ready for our mud masks," she said. Using just the tips of her fingers, she piled the greenish-blackish earth onto my cheeks and hers, easily spreading it around until only the whites of our eyes and pink from our lips showed. With mud-covered faces and towel-covered heads, we walked with great stature about the apartment, feeling like models or actresses before a big photo shoot.

"How about some tea?" Grandma always enjoyed the ceremony of making hot tea in the evenings. I loved picking out my favorite mug, each time choosing a different design. "Tea is so helpful for your immune system," she noted. Grandma always told me the facts about foods and herbs and how they worked and why. I appreciated how she treated me as a mature person. Grandma bought her green tea and other tea remedies in Chinatown, where her Chinese doctor practiced. "Come. I want to show you what Dr. Cheng gave me this time." Delicately, she untied a lovely silk cloth and opened it to reveal a folded piece of tightly woven burlap. Inside the material was a strange assortment of aromatic herbs and twigs. I can't remember exactly what she showed me; I was so consumed with wonder at the sight of the twisted roots and the smell of the oddly shaped leaves and seeds that I didn't pay attention to the names of them. Now, of course, I wish I had.

Grandma lit a candle and dimmed the lights as we moved to the sofa, sitting Indian style in our nightgowns beneath a blanket big enough for both of us to cuddle under. We wrapped our hands around our mugs, warming up as we tucked our nightgowns under our legs. Together, we shared "woman-to-woman" conversations about everything from movies, pigeons, artists, and cooking to boys, hair, travel, and family. The time flew by as the mud hardened, pulling our tight skin with it as it dried.

Another set of rinses and towel patting. Then, generously, Grandma doled white cream onto her fingertips and applied it onto the entire surface of my face. With soft music in the background, she covered me with a cozy blanket on the sofa and propped soft pillows under my neck and knees. She then whispered, "Close your eyes and relax," as she positioned cucumber slices over my eyelids.

Beauty night. Comfortable, cared for, and nourished. More than a looking-in-the-mirror beautiful, it was a custom that acknowledged beauty in a way that soaked deeply into the body, well below the skin. If you feel beautiful, you see beautiful.

my living will

Grandma's nurturing attitude motivated me to take better care of myself. A daily desire to make new choices was one of the ways I honored me. It was my strong yearning for change that assisted my intentions, bringing me to a space of center, balance, and ease. Once I chose change, I engaged my *will*—putting those choices and desires into action.

Will Power

Our *will* carries great power and is at our service. It is not dictating or demanding. Rather, it is an available resource, assisting us and helping us keep our intentions strong. It is something we can tap into and utilize at any given moment. As it rises up from our core, it supports us with its determination and drive. Grandma was willing to speak up and be vulnerable in many different arenas of her life. Her willingness created channels of openness, and from that openness, anything was possible.

Take some time to reflect on changes you envision. Give yourself realistic goals as you enter into this personal pact of living a new life. In the steady, continuous practice comes the change. Eventually, the resistance turns into persistence.

State Your Will

Saying "I will" is not forcing or demanding or whipping yourself into doing something, against which you might later rebel. It truly is an opening of a part of your being that lets in transformation. Summoning the spirit of willingness is a tool and an important step and focus for all of us.

I will exercise three times a week.

I will sit down and write for at least ten minutes a day.

I will organize one drawer or stack of papers today.

I will call a dear friend, just to check in and say "hi."

I will give up eating fried foods or candy or whatever food isn't best for me.

Surround Yourself with the Positive

Images of a well-kept closet, a great piece of art, or a favorite animal

Books about manifesting, persevering, and loving life

Quotes by great thinkers and dreamers

Words of encouragement and support

Music that inspires us and makes us sing

Friends who listen and share in our joys

Environments that allow us to practice change

Start a Small Streak

Count how many days in a row you can go without shopping.

Tally how many minutes you can exercise before stopping.

Note how long you can truly listen to someone without thinking of what you are going to say next.

See how many days you can add up without eating sweets.

Observe how many thoughts you can have that stay positive.

Spend ten minutes a day meditating, until your ten minutes turn into twenty.

Procrastinate on eating that donut. Instead, say, "I'll have one next time." And then repeat this action each time a donut is presented to you. Eventually, the next times will add up to weeks, months, and years.

Streak in Public

All of us have friends or family members who are *will*ing to cheer us on. Ask for help and then follow it. Just by telling others what our streak is, we create positive pressure.

Thy Will Be Done— Reward Yourself

Get a massage.

Buy a new book.

Listen to new music.

Take an hour to visit a bookstore.

Go to the park and swing.

Get new supplies for your hobby.

Go swimming.

Watch a movie.

Make your decision to change, and then follow through. It doesn't have to be a struggle. It doesn't have to be hard. Make it fun. Make it a game. You always have your will to assist and motivate you. As Grandpa Moore would say, "Keep it up, kiddo."

12
ON THE ROOFTOP

"Come, I want to show you something," Grandma said, as she dashed out the door of her apartment. I ran down the hall, following her up the side stairs to the rooftop. She pushed open the heavily weighted door with the entire side of her body. "This is my refuge," she told me.

The rooftop itself was nothing special—just a gray gravel roof, with a few concrete steps leading to a small, raised, covered deck in the center. At twelve, I wasn't too fond of heights, so I kept to watching the steps. One deep inhale from Grandma was all I could hear. And then I looked up.

We stood between the sky and the ground, overlooking the orange Golden Gate Bridge, leading to Sausalito with the blue Pacific Ocean below. I glanced quickly at the view of the Palace, surrounded by the lake, trees, neighboring homes, and apartment buildings. It was awe-inspiring. With her eyes closed, Grandma took in another deep breath. "I come up here to breathe in the fresh air and have my private time. I treat the rooftop as if it is my own, since no one else is ever around." She reached out her arms and lifted them with a big stretch.

I instantly had a vision of Barbra Streisand, spinning in a circle, with her arms out and chin held high. I looked at Grandma as the lyrics of "On a Clear Day You Can See Forever" played in my head. Her energy mimicked that same utter joy that traveled from her spirit, up through her chest, and out through her open hands, into the space above. Grandma seemed to be in her own little world.

She was more captivating than the view. Her body twirled, as she hugged herself with a full embrace. "Isn't the city beautiful from here?" she said. "This is where I come to meditate." I stood and stared. If positive energy could be seen, streams of her light would have been flying upward.

the joy of forgiveness

Have you ever been presented with an opportunity to feel what you hadn't been willing to feel before? Those stuffed emotions that dammed off your throat, blocked your breath, and stirred up your stomach? Those unexpressed feelings that had previously been suppressed and compressed somewhere down inside of you, rather than acknowledged and dealt with?

When old, locked-up feelings arise in our lives, we make a choice. We can react with a talk-to-the-hand attitude, stopping the feeling, dismissing it, and wistfully setting it aside. On occasion, though, when we feel strong enough and centered enough, we can let go of resisting the arising sensations. We can choose to sit with them, feel them, and go with the flow of emotions.

The mind needs permission to allow the entire "stack" of ignored feelings to come up. These blocked and locked feelings are the ones we didn't let ourselves feel at the time they actually occurred. They are the deeply seeded emotions of childhood disappointments, universal regrets, or unforgiving moments that we hang onto, consciously or unconsciously.

Recently, a forgiving opportunity showed up, allowing me to feel what had been suppressed for thirty years. With the upcoming event of my high school reunion, I felt a bubbling up of regretful memories and experiences with my boyfriend from that time. He and I had dated on and off all throughout high school, and thinking about him summoned an inner longing for forgiveness. As a teenager, I had always struggled with speaking up and communicating my true feelings that spanned from minor issues, such as where I wanted to eat, to much more important issues, such as jealousy and intimacy. Rather than addressing the subject, I went numb. I shut down every sensory response and became nonreactive.

He pried and tried to help me express myself; he was unsuccessful, which left him confused and angry. He asked me time and again to articulate my needs, and often the voice inside me screamed its desires, but no sound ever exited my mouth. Now the simmering memories in my soul's center heated to a thunderous longing for removal.

Judgments I had directed toward him in the past now seemed to reflect back toward me. All of the reasons I had believed valid for disliking him and his domineering manner had changed into understanding. The shame, the disappointment, the regret…I felt it all. At this outpouring of stacked emotions, all I could do was cry and recognize the words I hadn't said, the feelings I hadn't felt, and the observations I hadn't made. He was never to blame. It was never about him.

Eventually the stack lifted. I had a new appreciation for the value of perspective. I yearned for understanding and forgiveness for my immaturity. I felt my anguish of not speaking up, my anger at not knowing how, and his pain at my inability to converse. I felt a strong desire, above all, to recognize the truth and to live my truth going forward. And possibly, most importantly, I saw with new eyes. My perspective was now from a universal view of "one," rather than a personal view of "mine."

When we don't forgive, we hold ourselves and the other person in a negative space. Anytime we send pain, anger, judgment, dislike, cruelty, prejudice, and so on in the direction of another person, we create an environment of negativity. If those thoughts, feelings, and actions continue for long periods of time, then the undoing of them may take longer.

When your past emotions show up in your future, be prepared to sit down and allow the time necessary to go through the releasing process. As the memory arises, instead of stopping it and blocking it and disregarding it, because you know that it has caused you painful physical and emotional reactions in the past, take the time to say, "OK, I'm going to sit with it. I'm going to feel it and let it move through me, even though it is going to be difficult and uncomfortable." And when this happens, it isn't pretty. Actually, it is a complete mess. Thoughts dart across

Part 4

DELIVERED WITH LOVE

WORDS—

What is a book, anyway?

Just words.

Making sense of them is overrated.

Maybe words just want to be together,
like people we collect as friends or
items we collect as treasures.

Sometimes they have nothing in common
except that they are loved by the owner of that moment.

Words, like things, just want to be noticed.

Dots   hopeful   waterfall   tune   fringe

Roses   swerve   celestial   circle

The Too-Talented Seahorse

The Cloud Festival

The Cozy Blowfish

Words are great, any way we place them.

Hoo Rah!

13
CIAO, BELLA

"*Ciao, bella.*" Grandma's words bounced off the page. Reading her letters transported me directly to her apartment. I imagined her smiling and sitting at her dining room table with pen and pad, thinking about me and my life. "We would love you to visit. How is school going this year? What are you enjoying most? Today we thought of you as we were feeding the pigeons. Your favorite pigeons are still here." More than the obvious words of support and interest, I enjoyed the simple fact that she had taken time to write to me. I visualized her hand flowing with cursive, in tune with her joyful spirit, streaming across the sheets of paper. I felt her energy and affection come through the pages.

I wrote in return. For as long as I can remember, I have loved writing. As a child, filling out those basic handwriting workbooks and following the broken lines while creating the alphabet were my favorite after-school activities. While writing notes, the words themselves didn't even matter. It was the newness of being able to communicate independently that thrilled me. The way the pen glided along my stationary and the ink flowed onto the paper made me happy. Short two-and three-word sentences like, "How are you?" and "I'm fine," weren't earth-shattering; they didn't sound profound, but they came from a place of pure honesty and innocence.

Unlike any other form of message, there was, and is something genuinely heartwarming about receiving a handwritten letter or card in the mail. Every time I opened an envelope with my large, rolling, written address on the front from Grandma, I felt special. I felt worthy. I felt loved.

During my challenging years as a teenager, it was her constant care that compelled me to find a way out of my darkness. The ongoing agony of peer pressure, gossiping girls, and the overprotective boyfriend were overwhelming for me, a sensitive soul. I remember asking myself, "How would my grandparents feel if I wasn't alive?" Honestly, it was my vision of their pain that I grasped when I needed to get through my not-wanting-to-live days.

And those letters.

Often a letter would arrive on just the day that I would come home, teary-eyed, after a false rumor had been spread about me, or my boyfriend would be unexpectedly angry with me—most likely from that false rumor. Those letters from Grandma poured her love out on the page with her unyielding affection. "*Te amo, te amo*!" It was as though she knew that I was suffering silently and needed her words of encouragement. And near the end of each note, Grandpa would add a few lines of his own. "Hey, kiddo, keep it up!"

So I tried. I didn't want to cause them pain by giving up on my life or giving in to my depression, so I continued to write. This became my outlet for self-expression, or at least the amount of expression I could expose at that time. And it was through my writing that I found my soul's peace.

Everywhere I went, I wrote. I wrote about myself. I wrote about my feelings. I wrote about life. Writing became a space where I felt safe and comfortable to be me fully, without outside influences and judgments. My pens and paper became my most important and ever-present tools. Writing gave me an opening to share on a level deeper than I could do by voice. And although my grandparents and I talked by phone, it was the capacity to write that gave me the freedom I craved. In my letters, I found myself answering a constant call to be genuine and sincere. I yearned for clarity.

English words may never be able to equal the spiritual feelings we have as humans. I am sure that other languages, with their lyrical rolling of sounds, better match the energy in tune with the phrases. With her great Italian flair, Grandma Rosa spoke with her arms and hands and her entire body, reflecting her emotions. In love, people's chests expand and their shoulders roll back, as if to expose hearts even more with the words. And in anger, arms fly, elbows bend and fingers point. I have no problem deciphering the sentiments there. In English, though, the journey continues. Somehow, a universal language of the heart still desires to be unearthed.

please return

Ten years after Grandma died, Mom handed me a manila envelope. In it were many of the letters and cards I had written Grandma, which she proudly shared with family and friends. On the back of each note, she firmly reminded them to "please return."

After all these years, seeing my childhood letters reaffirmed her love for me. Not to mention the irony of the fact that although she usually didn't save anything, she cherished these letters as much as I did. And why did I receive them ten years instead of ten days after she died?

Maybe it was her way of sending a casual reminder to me: "Hello, honey, I am so glad you are writing this book. You have always loved to write. Here, look at all of these letters you wrote me. *Please return.*"

Many times I will simply sit and write a letter to me from Grandma or anyone else for that matter, dead or alive, as though we were having a conversation today. I start with a quiet space and a deep breath. I allow myself to trust whatever words come up, and then I just let the pen move. As I write, the voice I hear in my head sounds like my own, not Grandma's. The words like "hi honey" and "*ciao bella*" may even be coming from deep within my subconscious file of Grandma's favorite sayings, but nevertheless, the messages are meaningful and helpful.

I have found this practice useful not only in the words she expresses but also in the feelings attached to them. It always brings me a sense of calm reassurance that the place I am in and the emotions I am feeling are exactly what are important for me at this time. So why argue with it? Why not just have fun?

a letter from grandma moore, ten years after she passed

May 10, 2010

Before walking in to teach a high school yoga class, I sat in my car and reflected on my upcoming surgery. I wanted what was best, not only for my physical self, but also my spiritual and mental self. To add to that, all of the television stations were broadcasting news about the astronomical oil leak in the Gulf of Mexico. I watched with the world and cringed at the continuously streamed videos of oil funneling into the ocean.

Karen: Hi, Grandma

Grandma: Hi, honey

K: Could you ask some guides and angels to help us out here? We need to plug the oil leak and bless and clear the water. I also need help with my anxiety about my operation.

G: Sure, dear. If you can love what is taking place, you will be more peaceful. Love the Earth. Love the water. Love the oil. Instead of sending more negative energy in its direction, send love. And you, honey, love the opportunity to feel with your body. Love the process. Love the procedure. Love the wisdom and help. See it all with love.

K: Grandma, thank you for the signs. They really help. Do you have any other signs for me or stories to share?

G: They will continue to come to you. You know me. I'm always full of surprises. Right now we need you to feel better.

I paused in my writing and saw that the driver in the car in front of me had pulled away. As she'd had the only shady spot on the street, and the temperatures outside were reaching over one hundred degrees, I started my car to pull forward. On the radio played Grandma's signature song, "Just in time…and changed my lonely life that lovely day." *Grandma's here,* I sighed.

Her energy was undeniable. It infused the entire interior of my car, as though her spirit was sitting right there in the front seat next to me. I smiled more broadly and soaked up the fullness of the moment. The next song rang in, "Happy Days Are Here Again." Optimistic lyrics traveled through the car as Barbra Streisand belted it out. Again the message was crystal clear: "Happy days are here again!" It's a great feeling, being tied into the spiritual world and its possibilities. Joy is a beautiful way to live.

1969

Karen
5 years old

Dear Grandma
I Love you
Grandma Thank you for the
Cakarjacs. I Rate this
letter. I Love you so mace
that I im going to give you
a kis and a hag!

Love Karen

14

BRAVO!

"I've always been shyyyyyyyyyyy, I confess that I'm shy-yyyyyyyyy. Can't you guess that this confident air is a mask that I wear, 'cause I'm shy?" I stood downstage, house right, singing to an audience of empty chairs except for one—Grandma's. "Bravo!" rang out as her clapping ensued. There she sat, Indian style, front row center. Grandma had flown in to attend the entire last week of rehearsals and to watch me perform on Opening Night.

Ironically, I *was* shy. I knew I needed to learn how to speak up. So with Grandma in mind, I auditioned for our high school theater productions with the intent of finding my voice. During my senior year, I earned the lead role in *Once Upon a Mattress* as Princess Winifred—a girl who swam the moat, spoke her mind, and sang loudly about being "shyyyyyyyyyyy." As one who grew up timid and quiet, it took a lot of courage for me to not only try out for drama, but to build up the nerve to get out on stage. Up until that point, my theater experience consisted of a two-line ensemble role in *The Mouse That Roared*, a cheerleader in *Grease,* and a nonspeaking part as one of Fagan's thieves in *Oliver*.

Grandma loved the fact that I followed her mother's footsteps into musical theater. Renata Brunorini was asked to join the New York theater scene after she moved there in 1895. Her father, Antonio Brunorini, was the number one actor, playwright and comedian in Italy, so Mom says. Knowing this, local Italians begged Renata to perform and sing. For twenty-five years, she graced the stage, appearing in Italian operas and plays with her husband, Ettore, as director and translator. Actors crowded their home, reciting lines and rehearsing scenes. Perpetually pregnant, her body was always covered up by costumes—even when she played a nun. Grandma Rosa, the youngest of Renata's thirteen children, of whom only six survived, always played the part of infant or child when needed. She cherished her memories of growing up and being part of the ever-buzzing theater world.

And so, from an early age, Grandma inherited the gift of being an exuberant audience. Whether watching a musical or drama, amateur or professional, onstage or onscreen, she always gave "the show" her full attention. Her thrill for the arts was contagious. When I introduced her to our director, Mr. D., she responded with her most charming "*Ciao*," as she smiled broadly, holding his hands in hers. And then, drawing her thumb and forefinger across her lips, as though they were sealed shut, Grandma signaled that she would be very quiet for our rehearsal. Being quiet was a huge deal for Grandma.

Mr. D. knew about our family's history in the theater, which I happily shared before Grandma's arrival. He honored my request to have her sit in and reiterated that she was the *only one* allowed to watch what took place before opening night. Everyone else had to wait.

My friends fell in love with Grandma. She cackled loudly at each laughable moment, letting her voice be heard both front- *and* backstage. She made animated sighs and sounds of "Ahhh…" when appropriate, and always stood, clapped, and cheered with a big "*Bravo!*" at the end. Her relentless enthusiasm helped shape the space of confidence within us all, on the most often vulnerable stage. After each run-through, we walked off proud, confident, and prepared for our upcoming theater performance.

Opening night came, and the theater seats filled with an audience of family and friends. In my dress, drenched with water from "swimming the moat," I stood up and began my first lines of dialogue. My heart nearly pounded out of my chest. My voice sounded as though it were someone else's. I looked out into the closely packed crowd and saw Grandma. There she sat, Indian style, front row center, just as she had done for our rehearsals. I knew, from the joy on her face, there was no other place she would rather be.

In the midst of singing, I felt a sense of ease as I slipped into the character. Walking off, I still felt great. Yet, with every step back onto that stage, my nervousness returned. The moments spent on- and offstage felt equally exhilarating and terrifying. Each time, I looked to Grandma's smile for support and focused on her absolute delight at seeing me onstage. "The swamps of hoooomme are lovely to behooooold from far awaaaaay…"

I sang out. Everybody laughed. I found myself moving across the floor, sweeping my arms through the air and lifting my chin with each added verse.

We ended to a standing ovation and took our bows. Our show may not have been exceptional, but in Grandma's eyes, we couldn't fail. To her, "It was perfection. Bravo!"

I'm listening...

Tina and I went to lunch. Before we even sat down, Tina started singing the lyrics, "Getting to know you, getting to know all about you." The hair on the back of my neck stood up, chills spread down my thighs, and tears spontaneously welled up in my eyes.

"Your grandma is here," she pronounced. "She is wearing a vintage red dress with tights and is performing in *Carmen* on the other side and 'loving it.'"

The vision of Grandma in red seemed completely striking and "right on" to me. She would have *loved* acting on stage in one of her favorite classic operas. How great to imagine her performing and hearing "Bravo!" from her ethereal crowd.

face your fear list, or ready or not, here you come

As soon as we come into this world, we begin to be taught by our families what to like and dislike, what to say or not say, how to act or not act, and when to feel safe or unsafe. Fears are passed down without acknowledgment. The reactions of shrieking at snakes, of not looking over cliffs, or of losing self-control are imprinted energies that transfer from generation to generation.

One of my earliest childhood memories was one of fear. During a family gathering, at the young age of four, I was placed on the top of a tall ladder. With nothing to hold onto and no one to support me, I burst into tears. Everyone pointed and laughed at me while I gripped the edge, unable to help myself down. I felt confused and lost as to what to do and whom to trust. It was my first of many experiences of fear, which took me years to undo and understand. Inside, I knew that butterflies in my stomach and a heartbeat racing out of control were not universal feelings. So why was I scared? If I didn't take the time to work through these feelings, my fears would continue to hold me back from the full life I imagined for myself.

Another one of my early fears was pouring paint out of a can. Really. I felt embarrassed and silly for having such a phobia. Keeping things clean was my main objective when I was young, so I didn't paint for years for fear of making a mess. I watched others pour paint, eagerly and freely, without care about the drips down the sides or spots on the drop cloth. Their happy-go-lucky attitude toward all things that I feared sparked my interest. What did other people do or not do differently, and what was stopping me from overcoming my fears?

Fearful thoughts and stifled emotions hinder us from our creativity, our purpose, and our faith. Dammed-off energy and feelings develop into disease, pain, stress, and suffering.

Take a glance at your own life. Make a list of all of your fears. Write them down on a piece of paper, and then take a really good look at them. What rises inside of you? Do you feel self-conscious, alone, overwhelmed, or at a loss as to where to even begin? I invite you to approach the list with a sense of adventure and curiosity and then try new ways of facing your fears with fun and creative solutions.

My list of fears began as:

Horses

Heights

Speaking up

Saying the truth

People not liking me

Not being good enough

Losing control

Seeing my old boyfriend

Living

Unknown

Snakes

Singing in front of others

Hurting people's feelings

Exposing the true me to others

Going to a class with people I don't know

Once this list is made, take action to reduce it. Baby steps lead to bigger steps, which lead to self-acceptance and trust. Each step counts and strengthens, no matter how seemingly small. Start with something that feels possible, and then go from there.

Go to a stable and watch horses…take horseback riding lessons.

Step up on a stool to reach higher…step up on a ladder to paint.

Sign up for a watercolor class…go to the watercolor class.

Sing out loud around your house…sing in front of a friend.

Look through a book about snakes…visit a pet store and watch snakes.

Close your eyes and sit with the unknown…meditate in silence every day.

Make a conscious effort to open yourself to the idea of change. Summon the Universe to present you with opportunities to overcome your fears. One friend always asked for growth at a gentle pace, a pace that perfectly matched her spirit. And that's what she got—gentle, fun, inventive ways to challenge her and to explore. Other friends enjoyed eliminating obstacles in dramatic ways, and that's what they got—big boulders of transformation through divorces, job losses, or economic changes.

Fear can be a welcome visitor. It can offer good information and be a great motivator. I ask myself why I am afraid. I quickly understand my present purpose. Fear is the greatest indicator of what I need to do next in this lifetime, for facing fears illuminates a path toward inner freedom and personal peace.

If you step up to the plate of life and swing away at your fears, one at a time, what you will find is more delight in the steps taken to face them, more relief from not holding back, and a good laugh along the way with each attempt. Have fun with it. As Tina and I once said simultaneously, "If you're not afraid of anything, then you're not living!"

15
WHEN LIGHTNING STRIKES

The storm crept closer as I tried to sleep. This wasn't just your usual scattered showers and distant thunderstorm. This was a full-fledged strong-winded, torrential downpour.

Just hours before, after finishing the outdoor restoration of our home, Kelly and I had gone to bed with feelings of a job well done. Earlier that afternoon, we'd taken in the beauty of our new retaining wall, brick patio, curved concrete pathway, hummingbird-friendly landscaping, and built-in spa. We "oohed" and "aahed" as we plugged in the hot tub for the first time. Sounds of bubbling water tingled our eardrums and released our tensions, immediately relaxing us. Finally, our project was complete. It had taken months of dreaming, sketching, visualizing, planting, organizing, and trusting to create such a sanctuary. I had acted as contractor while still teaching yoga, painting at my art studio, and taking care of our four school-aged children. We felt relieved and thrilled, eager to enjoy the view of city lights and the night's sky.

And then the storm arrived.

I kept waking up, thinking, *I hope everything is all right out there. I hope the plants can hold up. I really hope the storm doesn't damage our new hot tub.*

When the crashing bolts closed in directly above us, my thoughts moved to my precious computer. Yes, I had it plugged into a filtered surge strip, but I didn't completely rely on its protection for my valued files. I looked at the clock—4:40 a.m. I knew it was too early to get up, but I just couldn't take the chance.

I nudged Kelly in bed and told him my concerns. Still deep in his sleep, he shrugged and turned away, mumbling under his breath, while I sat up and stepped into my slippers. Pouring rain pelted the windows and ground outside, as I drowsily made my way downstairs to our office next to the kitchen. I stood at the corner of my desk, ready to reach down toward the computer plug, when I heard a voice in my head say, "Scream."

Scream? I thought. *I don't scream.* Then I heard the voice again, this time loud and clear: "Scream!"

Immediately, I placed my hands over my ears, closed my eyes, and did just that—I screamed! One long, thunderous crack hit. Lightning struck the palm tree directly outside the office window. The charge ran through my body as the sound and vibration shuddered throughout our house, blowing out the glass panes behind my desk. The boom was so intense that my kids woke up and rushed out of their rooms.

"Mom, are you OK?" Christopher asked when he found me, with my ears still covered. I stood motionless, stunned at the sight of the room around me. Shattered bits of glass flickered everywhere. The curtain blew wildly around. Rain streamed inside the now-absent window.

It felt like forever as I stood in a frozen position. During that time, I quickly repeated the past chain of events over and over again in my head. What just happened? And then it came to me.

Had I not listened to the order to scream, certain parts of my body would have undoubtedly been harmed. The air I released kept me from inhaling the miniscule particles from our single-pane, out-of-date windows. Because of this, they shattered into tiny, glitter-like pieces which scattered in all directions. My eyes had been closed, so the glass couldn't scratch them. By covering my ears with my hands, I obviously took care of my delicate ear canals. Had I not screamed and sent out my own sound waves, the intense pressure most likely would have caused hearing damage, not to mention the possibility of inhaling thousands of glass specks into my lungs.

Christopher came over to where I was standing. "Are you OK?" he asked again.

"Yes," I answered this time, still in shock.

I wondered why, out of all of the times that I had the opportunity to check on things through the night, why did I decide to get up just then? How amazing is it that I would be standing in that place, on that day, at that moment?

Kelly clamored downstairs to the dining room, yelling, "Come here and help me out." The storm, the broken glass, the rain gushing into our house had obviously wakened him as well. He was completely unaware of the fact that I had gotten up just a short while earlier and had been standing right next to the window in the office. He quickly ran for towels and a broom to soak up the puddles and clean up the mess. I couldn't move or answer him. Kelly ran out of the house to see where the lightning had struck. Just outside our office space, our date palm tree had burst into flames leaving a charred check mark where the strike had hit. Fortunately, the rainwater had begun dousing the fire, but the tree, now black and smoldering, sent billowing smoke and the burnt smell of its trunk streaming into the house.

In the midst of the downpour, Kelly had somehow heard a high-pitched noise coming from the side of our home where the gas meter was located. The dial was spinning out of control. We now had a burning tree *and* a gas leak. Not a good combination. We rushed out front with our children, all in pajamas, and waited for the gas company to answer the phone. "Get out of the house!" they warned. "We will send a technician out as soon as possible. Stay outside until he gets there."

Within minutes the technician arrived and turned off the main line to our home. As the sun began to rise, we went back inside to assess the damages. Kelly hurried downstairs. Windows were shattered in my art studio, family room, and the dining room as well. Rainwater had soaked the carpet and floors, and the bits of glass extended everywhere.

I walked toward the kitchen and stopped. Fallen from a shelf on the floor in front of me—one red rose. I reached down, picked it up, and turned toward the shattered dining room windows. The glass had cracked and broken into the shape of a perfectly defined heart! All I heard inside my head were Grandma's words: "It's OK, honey. Everything is going to be fine. Although this may seem terrible, it isn't. We are all watching over you, and everything will turn out beautifully."

Immediately, I had a split-second knowing of an overlapping message. It sounded like it came from the same guided voice that alerted me to scream, although this time, the words were calm and expressive. "God is thrilled that you finished remodeling the area on the side of the house, but he really wants the *entire* home, including the backyard and pool, to be completed. This was necessary and helpful for that to happen."

I sighed.

In my head I replied, "Do I understand this correctly? This divine thunderstorm that broke our windows, burned our tree, and broke our gas line was a gift?"

"Exactly," I heard.

The palm tree that burned down equaled the cost of our deductible, so the insurance company covered all of the related expenses and paid for the replacement of our entire backyard walkway of concrete. They also paid for new windows, which obviously needed to be updated, and a new gas line, which, unbeknownst to us, was a hazard as well. It had been encased in PVC pipe and was not up to code. Period. All of these unknown factors that put us at risk could have caused great harm.

Miraculous events take place every day. I always pray that God will use me in a positive and purposeful way, and I know that one of my purposes in this lifetime is to bring beauty to what desires to be beautiful. Sometimes, gifts come wrapped in "striking" packages.

the gong

A wise friend, Fr. Gil Martinez, once shared a story with me. On the night prior to visiting the pope at the Vatican, he set an alarm clock before going to bed, yet woke up early, before it went off. While he was getting ready, it softly chimed, "Dun, dun, dun, dun…dun, dun, dun, dun."

So as not to wake any other visitors, he tried to turn the clock off, but to no avail. He continued to get dressed until five minutes later, "Dun, dun, dun, dun…dun, dun, dun, dun." This time the bells were a little louder, but again, he couldn't turn off the alarm.

Another five minutes passed and then it sounded louder still. "*Dun, dun, dun, dun…dun, dun, dun, dun.*" Now he was getting frustrated. He couldn't figure out how to stop the alarm.

Then five minutes later, as blaring as a gong, "DUN, DUN, DUN, DUN…DUN, DUN, DUN, DUN!" The alarm was too loud too ignore and had his complete attention.

Sometimes we receive warning signs similar to that of the gong. They begin with a whisper in our ear, the gentle chiming voice guiding us, "Maybe that's not a good idea." Then the low voice gets a little bit louder: "Are you sure you want to go there?" Each time help gets our attention in louder ways— lost keys, a speeding ticket, a discouraging comment, a cavity, self-loathing.

I can think of so many soft, gentle-voiced first alarms given to me. "Maybe you should call later. Now is not the best time. Sunscreen would be a good idea. It might be time to clean the vent to the refrigerator. You may want to have your tires checked. Call and check in with your mom today. You ought to go to the doctor's for a physical. A walk outside in nature would be calming." These random thoughts, sweet reminders and suggestions come to us, hoping to help ease our days.

When we don't listen to the wisdom, we get secondary warnings and insights. These get a bit more of our attention: indigestion, arguments, a pulled muscle, a burned-out refrigerator, a flat tire, a root canal, sunburns. All of those frustrating energies take our time away from what we love to do and cost us more monetarily, emotionally, physically, and energetically.

If we allow the alarm to continue to ring, the next level of distress signals occur—drug use, alcohol abuse, loss of friendships, depression, isolation, separation, marital affairs.

Eventually, without awareness and focused action, the gong goes off. It is that "Now I have your full attention" message, which may come in the form of a disease, unemployment, divorce, homelessness, estrangement, obesity, alcoholism, drug addiction, incarceration, or car accident.

These Universal timeouts are God-given breaks, which help us reassess where we are, what we are doing, and how we are spending our time and energy. When we get ahead of ourselves or miss an important opportunity for growth, the Universe itself steps in and creates the space for our reflection. And yes, it may come in the form of the flu, a canceled flight, or a job change.

Whether we like it or not, the lessons continue to present themselves. Better to choose to listen and act than wait for the gong to go off. But if the alarm does sound, just close your eyes, place your hands on your heart, and say, "I am sorry. I love you." Help is on its way.

everything is a gift

The next time a seemingly negative situation arises, see if you can recognize and accept it as a blessing rather than a curse. See if you can find the gifts in what may be camouflaged as issues, mistakes, problems, or illnesses.

What disagreement wasn't an obvious opportunity to speak up for yourself?

What speeding ticket wasn't a clear message to "slow down and be safe," whether we wanted to believe we were getting ahead of ourselves or not?

What action of saying something hurtful wasn't an opening to forgive yourself and others?

What minor heart attack wasn't a wake-up call?

When wasn't bed rest a time for contemplation, for catching up on reading materials, or for watching movies you missed?

Take the time to see things from opposite angles, colorful views, and humorous outlooks. Then receive all the gifts as they present themselves.

Part 5

"NEW YORK,
NEW YORK"

DREAM–

I am in a bathroom with Kelly.

I hear a loud banging on the outside of the door.

Someone is pushing on the door and trying to get in.

*Scared, I force the door closed, hoping
the stranger will leave.*

*I plead to Kelly for help, and he hurries
over, barricading the door with me.*

*Using my entire body to try to keep the door closed,
I feel anxious and terrified, not knowing who is outside.*

*My dream suddenly changes perspectives,
from the view inside the bathroom to a
view from the outside, looking in.*

*It is the same scene, only this time,
I see that I am the one
pushing the door, trying to get in.*

I am the one I feared.

16

SEPTEMBER 11, 2005

One Sunday morning, Kelly and I entered St. Patrick's Cathedral during one of our regular trips to New York City. I reached over for the daily bulletin, as I tilted my head back, gazing at the remarkable features of the church's interior. We walked toward the altar and sat down on the creaky wooden pew. Once seated, I looked down at the bulletin: "September 11, 2005." I felt stunned that I hadn't been aware of the date sooner. Earlier that morning, we woke up and felt drawn to visit the World Trade Center site, not knowing that this was indeed the anniversary of its devastation four years prior. After mass, we approached the red double-decker touring bus, for our first-ever tour ride. The city was beaming with people in bright-colored, late-summer clothing, walking to shops, dashing to classes, and rushing to jobs. Shared historical accounts about the city's past industry and constant change took us back through time.

After several stops, we arrived at the sacred place, now a flat land of dirt and trucks, and paid homage along with everyone around us. We stood outside the chain-link fence and quietly looked out over the scene. The energy felt sad but light at the same time. So many prayers had obviously helped lift the darkness and dust. Strength and perseverance predominated. It seemed as though the citizens, as a whole, had decided not to allow the tragic events of September 11, 2001, to identify them with pity. The city itself felt positive, purposeful, and clean.

We left the dirt area and walked toward a small stone chapel next to where the World Trade Center had stood. It doubled as a respite for so many that day and the days that followed. We had coincidentally arrived during a special memorial mass, in time to hear the priest share his accounts from that day back in 2001.

A woman whispered, "Here is a memento brochure for you," as she literally pulled us inside, handing us the program for the day's commemoration. Once we were standing inside, the atmosphere felt thick and dense. Our feet were glued to the floor, our bodies frozen.

On the walls hung banners of children's drawings, with handprints and flags of hope. Earlier that week, I had discovered photographs of those same mementos in a visitor's guide to New York. I was drawn toward the stories and photos of this particular chapel—the chapel that, although very near to the Twin Towers, had been left standing. In the spaces around the perimeter, displays of firefighters' clothing and letters from schoolchildren filled glassed-in window boxes. Family members and friends of deceased loved ones filled the aisles. Feelings of respect and humility permeated the space. As the service progressed, I found myself silently offering prayers of gratitude for the honor and blessing of being brought to such a place on such an emotional day. When the final verse of the ceremony's song played, the music transported us and the heaviness outside.

Quietly, we made our way toward the street. Kelly sat on the curb for a short while, composing himself. A mother and her teenage daughter sat down near him, leaning their heads together, holding long-stemmed red roses. People everywhere carried roses, setting them at the edge of the fenced area as a tribute to their relatives and coworkers. We needed some time to just be outside. Soon, though, I looked up and noticed the activity across the street. Workers walked gladly. Taxis flashed by us. Mothers pushed strollers. The city was alive.

We walked back to the bus, feeling inspired and pleased to be a powerful part of the city's healing. As the bus traveled down the road, I noticed a street sign: Moore Street. "Hey. Look at that," I told Kelly. I then glanced above the sign, and on the wall in giant five-foot bold red letters was—R O S A.

My mouth dropped. I showed Kelly both signs. "Look. R-O-S-A on Moore Street. What are the chances of that?" We went around the corner, and I noticed that ROSA was part of the word ROSARIO'S—a restaurant in the financial district. It was only because a wall blocked it, at the exact angle where we had stopped, that we could read it as ROSA. Incredible.

Moore Street—New York City

I'm listening...

Rosario's Deli was located at 38 Pearl Street, which intersects Moore Street in New York City. The restaurant closed in 2008.

Once I arrived home from that trip, I e-mailed this moving story about September 11 to a few close friends. After I clicked "send," I noticed the time...9:11 a.m. Instantly my heart pounded, my hands shook, and huge tears welled in my eyes. God is so good.

why wait?

People turn tragedies into triumphs all the time. They create foundations and blogs in memory of their loved ones. They raise money to fight diseases and walk miles together to fund treatments. When it comes to facing challenges, people are moved, inspired to make a difference in the world. I have always admired the courage and tenacity of those who overcome such pain. I have to ask, though: Why wait for a tragedy to do something extraordinary? Why not do something spectacular *now*?

Signing up to teach yoga to girls in prison and stepping up on top of a ladder to paint a tall ceiling are collectively revered as triumphs in my life. Over and over, the "whys" turned into "why not's"! What are we really waiting for? Simply sharing knowledge, camaraderie, and compassion are profound ways of giving back.

Have you turned tragedies into triumphs in your life?

How have you been inspired to act in an extraordinary way?

What small step can you make today, toward a personal or community goal?

17

ENCHANTED APRIL

After an hour's wait at the half-price ticket center in Times Square, Courtney and I stepped up to the ticket counter. "We would like four tickets to *Take Me Out*, the baseball play. I heard it received rave reviews."

"You do know that there is full frontal male nudity in this show," the ticket salesman pronounced. His eyes focused solely on Courtney, at age twelve, with a look of "Not a good idea," and "Really? You can't be serious." He then turned and stared right back at me. He may not have actually said those words out loud, because I was so stuck on the "full frontal male nudity" part; it's hard to say for sure. What I did know is that we needed another show choice—fast.

Kelly, who was standing just outside the line, read a quick review about a play called *Enchanted April*. "Let's see something new," he said. "Something we wouldn't normally try. This play was up for lots of awards, and it looks good." In a split-second decision, I blurted out, "Four tickets to *Enchanted April*." He gave us a nod and said, "Good choice," as he handed us our tickets. Immediately Kelly began doubting himself. "I shouldn't have said anything. What if it turns out to be bad? What if we don't like it?" He didn't want the responsibility of choosing the show. In those days, he didn't want to influence any of the choices that could keep him from my good graces.

During the previous six months, Kelly and I had hit a point in our twenty-year marriage where we were ready to face some hard truths. Unhappy, I was searching for my life's purpose, self-love, and a more authentic love with Kelly. We consulted a marriage counselor and were working on communicating more honestly and on changing old patterns. We had stripped our relationship to the studs and were building it back up, one block at a time. "I didn't want to make that decision," he reiterated. "I told myself I wouldn't do that." Our conversations had become opportunities to practice consideration. During that time, we were making it a habit to carefully think out each decision before expressing it out loud. I assured him that his choice would be fine. Truthfully, none of us had a better one to offer.

After riding back to our hotel, we waited for Mom's taxi to arrive out front. She had just flown in to join us for a few days of our vacation. When we told her about the show tickets, she threw her arms up and exclaimed, "Oh, *Enchanted April*! It will be wonderful."

"Really?" I said. This was a play that I wasn't too familiar with.

"Oh, yes. Mother used to watch this film over and over. It was one of her favorites."

After setting Mom's luggage upstairs in her room, we hurried to the theater for the matinee performance. Sitting on what was left of a cushion in the cab, we sped through the city streets. Soon we arrived at the theater at 111 West 44th street.

"Forty-four," I exclaimed. This number has always carried great symbolic meaning in my life. I see it as a sign that the angels are guiding, helping, and watching over me. It is a milepost of sorts, saying, "You are on the right track."

"Oh!" Mom clapped her hands in front of her heart as we pulled up to the theater. "The Belasco Theater is where Grandma used to play as a young girl, while her mother, Renata, performed there. She used to tell me stories about being at this theater all the time. It was a great accomplishment to be onstage at the Belasco."

People were gathered outside and filing into the foyer of the theater, which had been originally named the Stuyvesant Theater. It had later been renamed the Belasco Theater in 1910 by David Belasco, a native San Franciscan and famous playwright, who wrote *Madame Butterfly* and *Girl of the Golden West.* Altogether, Belasco wrote over forty plays that were made into movies.

With the change of name came Tiffany lighting, ceiling panels, rich woodwork, and sprawling murals by American artists. The theater included a ten-room duplex penthouse apartment that Belasco used as both his living quarters and office space. Technically, it was outfitted with the most advanced stagecraft tools available, including extensive lighting rigs, a hydraulics system, and a vast wing and fly space. The theater still operates with much of the original decor today.

After being escorted to our seats, we read biographies of the cast in the Playbill and took in the scene. On the stage hung a full curtain, which displayed an ad from the *London Times* for a villa in Northern Italy. The date read February 13, 1922. "Grandma would have been twelve then," Mom said. "This is the same age as you are now, Courtney. And Renata, Grandma's mother, most likely performed here in 1922 at the time the play is set."

Of course, she would have performed there, with her long history in the theater. Courtney leaned over and whispered, "Wouldn't that be something, if one of the character's names was Rose?" The lights dimmed as the show began:

> Lottie Wilton appears first. She is in search of a getaway from the noise and dreary weather and atmosphere of London. While turning in her application for the villa's rental, she meets another woman who introduces herself…"Rose."

Our eyes darted toward each other's. In unison we gasped. I grabbed the sides of my seat, holding on for what was to come.

> Lottie and Rose, both married, yet looking like widows, live joyless lives in London. They decide to rent an Italian villa bathed in sunlight and wisteria on the Mediterranean. They travel by train to the country house, making a stop in Genoa.

"Genoa!" Chills ran down my legs and arms as my heart rate quickened. Genoa is where Renata was born and a place which Grandma spoke of with such fondness. Rose *and* Genoa! *Something is definitely happening here.*

After a few weeks of fresh air and reflection, Lottie begins to feel light and full of joy. She guides Rose into inviting their successful, yet self-absorbed husbands, who can't understand what could possibly cause their wives to spend time away from them, to join them at the villa.

Rose shared much of the same sadness and yearning for more love and fulfillment from her husband that I felt. And her husband's philosophy of "Later, we can spend time together," completely reflected Kelly's previous attitude.

Concerned and confused, the husbands arrive at the cottage. Suddenly they see beauty in their wives, as though being awakened from a fog. Almost magically, the men and women reignite their love and affection for one another.

Hypnotized by this display, we took in the words, the conversations, the interactions. Our story as of recent months was being exhibited onstage, right before our eyes. We continued to follow the blossoming of the characters, now completely aware of their image mirrored to our own. The couples radiated with the beauty and love that they already possessed, yet with a new appreciation for each other.

It felt as though Grandma had directed the entire storyline of events just for Kelly and me, with Mom and Courtney as our witnesses. In the final phrase of the final scene, Lottie shares, "Sometimes we have to take one step back in order to move forward." I cried. Kelly cried. Mom and Courtney cried. The theater emptied.

Now, if you ventured outside my home through the courtyard and down to our pool area, you would see three plum-colored canvas cabanas surrounded by various shrubs and queen palms. In between the cabanas along the back wall are heavenly green wisteria vines, in memory of our day of *Enchanted April*. A description I once read said, "Wisteria vines climb by twining their stems around any available support."

Every time I see them, I think of that profound message from above. Their soft, swaying leaves and seasonal dangling clusters of purple flowers remind me to slow down, count my blessings, and take time for a sweet kiss or hug on the step with Kelly. They say, "Remember *Enchanted April*. Don't lose sight of your wonderful marriage and happy life. And don't take it for granted."

I'm listening...

While looking through my e-mail inbox, I read, "It's almost time. Are you ready?" It was sent to me from Wisteria, a catalog company. Of course Wisteria would send me a message today, the symbol of Grandma being our support. It arrived on the eve of my daughter, Kristina, checking into the hospital for her baby's delivery.

on many levels

An experience of one profound moment in time, such as the day we spent at *Enchanted April*, happens on a very deep level. But just how many levels affect us simultaneously? What if we could accept each level as equally important to our growth? Is it even possible to be aware of all of these levels? Real, imaginary, direct, indirect, future, past, healing, ethereal, symbolic, personal, universal, emotional, spiritual…the list goes on.

I sit and watch the play with my legs crossed on the soft red velvet cushion, holding the glossy-paged Playbill, breathing in the scent of cologne from the gentleman sitting next to me. I imagine angels, guides, and loved ones gently leading us along and comforting us as our story unfolds, noting how closely it relates to my marriage, yet glimpsing a hopeful upcoming time with Kelly, better than the relationship we now share. I feel vulnerable, reliving my past mistakes and agonizing choices; yet, with each new perspective, I feel them dissipate and transform to a higher frequency. Simultaneously I sense a magical healing of energy move in and through me, renewing what was pained. Italy, Rose, 44th Street. It's as though the entire play was written, produced, and directed with me in mind, with the mystery of knowing and not-knowing equally balanced. I feel unattached to this body, time and place. A tingling of my soul vibrates with sensations of utter peace and joy.

All levels in sync with what is divine. All levels happening at once. If we only understood how supported we truly are.

Pick a memorable moment in your life and write down all of the levels you experienced.

Are there new levels not listed that add to your life events?

What levels are you open to receiving that you have yet to experience?

I'm listening...

How many people were in cahoots with this experience at *Enchanted April*?

Grandpa Moore, throwing us a curve ball with the baseball play, *Take Me Out*. Great-Grandma Renata, choosing the Italian Belasco Theater, where she performed. Grandma Rosa, directing each step of the storyline, bringing light to our loving relationship. Kelly's guide giving him the nudge to choose the play, most likely whispering in his ear, "*Enchanted April* is the one for you." My guide, keeping me preoccupied as I stepped up to the counter, so sure of what I selected, only to be shocked and at a loss for what show to choose next. Courtney's guide, who whispered, "Rose will be here," so we didn't miss one moment of their well-laid-out plan. Mom's guide, bringing her along, not only to witness the event, but to share the historical details and memories that needed to be noted.

Sometimes we just have to sit back and enjoy the "coincidences" that are planned for us.

18

THREE GENERATIONS

"Three generations!" Grandma exclaimed loudly to the taxi driver, as she patted his shoulder, pulling herself forward from the backseat. We started laughing, feeling slightly embarrassed, yet thrilled at her determination to take charge. "Really? I wouldn't have thought that," he responded.

We all had "great Italian genes," Grandma would say. I, age twelve, with my petite stature, olive skin, and hazel eyes, and my mother with her elegant long, dark hair, wrinkle-free forehead, and just-right nose. Grandma's youthful energy, soft smooth skin, and gorgeous high cheekbones always received compliments. No one believed that *she* was a grandma.

This was the first time just the three of us traveled together. In three days, we saw five Broadway shows: two matinees and a production again each evening. Strolling through historic neighborhoods, eating at popular delis, and meandering through unique boutiques kept us entertained during the between-show hours. We walked so much that my happily weary feet throbbed at the end of the night. Completely exhausted, yet still energized, I couldn't sleep. I lay awake in bed at the Hotel Wales, listening to the traffic go by at two, three, even four in the morning. The noise, the busyness, the activity—it was all so awakening. This was to be my introduction to New York City and to a life beyond my own.

East-coasters, and especially Manhattanites, move fast, like a freight train on holiday. I, on the other hand, am from Tucson. Similar to Maui time, Tucson time is unhurried. Maybe it's the dry heat, which wears on us and slows us down, or maybe it's our close proximity to Mexico, with its "siesta" attitude just across the border. Or it could be the fact that most of our residents are retired transplants, who have neither pressing agendas nor specific timelines to abide by. Either way, there is a definite lifestyle here, which is slow and steady. From Tucson to New York City, I had to gear up.

While we walked through Times Square, Grandma reached for Mom and me and pulled us close to her side. "Just feel the excitement and the buzz," she said, locking her arm under mine. I could feel the shift in her energy. With her help, we took on the attitude of "I belong here. I know what to do. I know where I'm going." Grandma's big-city confidence provided relief from the constant noise and nudging of bodies.

She was so proud of her birthplace that she just bounced through every step. "Washington Park was right around the corner from where we lived." It felt as though she had plugged into her roots of the city. "I used to walk to the Italian bakery by myself to buy bread and take the bus to the theater. Arthur, my brother, and I used to play stickball in the streets with the other kids. We had such fun growing up here," she said, as she smiled her way across town.

Her enthusiasm emanated as she spoke about her life as a young girl. Taking each second as an opportunity, she instilled the power in us to be sharp, strong, and independent. And now, as the experienced elder, she passed on her wisdom to Mom and me—like how to hail a cab, for starters.

Grandma asked me to stand in front, believing that my youthful charm would get the attention of a quick-moving driver. "Hold your arm up high, dear, so that they can see you," she yelled, from a good distance away. A sudden swerve after a short wait—it worked every time. While telling the driver our destination, she spoke directly and matter-of-factly, so they wouldn't take us on an "extra ride."

Once in the cab, Grandma leaned in toward the middle and went into her usual spiel. Stories, achievements, and honors about all of her children and grandchildren flooded out. Heck, she shared this with just about anyone who would listen. And if you drove a cab…well, let's just say that taxi drivers became her captive audience. Every time we "cabbed it," the three of us would scoot into the backseat, and then, quickly leaning forward, Grandma would boast loudly again, "Three generations!" Every time.

the grid of time

Years ago, after Grandma passed, while meditating; I received a vision of time. I was shown time as an endless grid of sparkling energy—above, below, on the same plane, angled, forward, backward—all time being "*now*." Every experience happening at the same time. Not earlier or later. Not before or after. Just, simply, all time being present.

And the idea of time seemed to be elastic and vibrant, with a constant flow of energy. The times we create in our mental awareness are always shifting and molding into new concepts and new experiences, based on the constant changes of our own experience and understanding.

Isn't it interesting that when a friend is thinking of us, we exist in his or her mind at that time? Yet we may neither be aware of the thoughts nor have the knowledge of our being there. And if many people are thinking of us, do we not exist in many places at the same time?

We may never know how intricately we are all connected on this earth. We may never know just how many divine happenings have come together solely for our benefit of learning, exploring, living, and growing. We may never know how magnificent our spirits are, unless we open our minds to the idea of just that. And if time doesn't exist in the way we have believed, then what is the purpose of time?

It keeps our thoughts and feelings organized in smaller fractions, so that we can collect more thoughts and feelings. It is our way of wrapping up an idea, so it doesn't get lost or overwhelm us. We use time to communicate about the accumulation of events, emotions, traumas, growth periods, and everyday moments that make up our life experience. It brings a comparative framework to our lives and within the collective community of others. But what happens when we step away from the framework we have created? We see that time itself is continuous and ever-changing. It does not begin one day and end the next. Only the structure of time changes—which we, ourselves, placed on it. There are no boundaries or limits, only opportunities in time.

How do you look at time? Do you always have "plenty of time," or do you find that there is "never enough time"?

Does the clock or watch dictate what time it is, or do you listen to your inner guidance system, keeping you in time?

I'm listening...

I helped Mom move into her new townhome recently. The sweet lady neighbor from next door stopped by to introduce herself. "You moved in just in time." They were finally completing the pool after months of work and the workmen and trucks were no longer there. Mom said, "This is Dollie and this is Gracie." Her two lhasa apso's trotted over to smell the scent of their new friend. I asked the neighbor if she had any pets. "No," she said, "just roses." Hello, Grandma.

Part 6

TRAVELING TOGETHER

FAMILY –

We all have an innate desire to belong.

*From the moment our umbilical cord is cut,
we make every effort to reconnect to our roots.*

*Instinctively, we want to know where we
came from and who came before us.*

*Even when family isn't physically present in our
daily lives, we spend time thinking about, talking
about, or experiencing feelings about them.*

*Family often plays the seemingly difficult role of
"catalyst"—the ultimate teachers who shape us into
truth-seeking, purpose-fulfilling, genuine individuals.*

*Playing these roles is not an easy task, but
it is the greatest gift one can offer.*

And why wouldn't our families be our greatest teachers?

They are the ones we spend the most time with.

*Whether in person, in thought, or in
spirit—relatives never leave us.*

*And when we truly think about the meaning of family,
we know that we are always connected.
We are all one.*

19

THE BOAT

While living in San Francisco, my grandparents owned an old light blue 1968 Dodge Monaco. Grandpa had purchased it new—a full-sized sedan of grand proportions, with signature delta-shaped tail lamps, which filled the entire length of their garage from tip to tip. Grandpa said he always had to "kiss the wall" so that the car would fit and the garage door could close. It was so long in fact, that I referred to it as "the Boat."

One time when Mom, my two daughters, and I were visiting, we decided to take the Boat out on a drive through the city. Grandpa came down and directed as Mom pulled the car forward and back, just so, without bumping into the walls or corners of the garage. I shook my head and cringed, wondering if this was such a smart idea.

I watched Mom wrestle the wheel with both hands and arms, due to the lack of power steering. Kimberly and Kristina jumped into the back, which could have fit five people across...*easily.* I sat in front on the mint green, leather-covered bench seat, across from Mom. There was literally a full arm's length between us.

"Where do you park the Boat?" I jokingly asked Mom, while looking for a longer-than-usual parking space at Fisherman's Wharf. Honestly, the car was so long, we finally surrendered to the boat's abnormality, and settled for a spot on a remote side road, and walked.

After a full day of outings, we made our way home. Mom asked, "Shall we take Lombard?"

"Lombard?" I questioned, not knowing the streets of San Francisco.

"Yes," Mom replied. "*Lombard.*"

"Uh oh." It finally registered. Lombard—universally known as the curviest road in the world. Many people like to say that they have driven down Lombard when they come to visit San Francisco. And now my adventuresome mom wanted to drive the Boat down Lombard as well.

The kids in the backseat started cheering, "Let's do it! Let's do it!" Mom lined up in the queue behind a few other cars. By this point, the girls were bouncing and rooting Mom on, leaning up on the front seat. Their voices rose with anticipation. The Boat took up nearly the entire length of road between twists.

"Turn...turn...*turn!*" we all hollered together. Mom maneuvered that wheel, hand over hand, with all of her strength, to get it going in the right direction. Just as she was able to straighten it out, she had to start reaching over, fist over fist, turning it the opposite way. Its turning radius equaled eight to one. Eight rotations of the wheel for one turn. Every time she pointed the car in a new direction, we cheered her on with unprompted clapping.

Once at the bottom, we caught our breath and pinched our cheeks for relief. Exhausted from laughing, we pulled up to Grandma's apartment building. Mom parked on the street, deciding it would be best to let Grandpa pull the Boat into the garage. Good choice.

The girls raced upstairs, still reeling from our escapade. "How was your day?" Grandma asked. We told her how much fun we had visiting Alcatraz, Fisherman's Wharf, and Ghirardelli Square. Grandma hugged us and said, "Oh that sounds like a wonderful day."

The day we took The Boat out in San Francisco.

Then Mom chimed in casually, "Yes, and Lombard."

"Oh, that's great, honey," Grandma replied, and then paused. "*Lombard!*" she gasped. "You did *what*?" We all burst out laughing once more.

unreasonable

I have been unreasonable my whole life. Or, at least, that is what everyone has been telling me.

Going on a goodwill mission to Iran with the Champion's Club at the age of thirteen.

Getting married at the age of eighteen.

Starting a family at the age of nineteen.

Acting as PTA president at the age of twenty-four.

Buying an "on-the-market-forever" home, which no one else wanted.

Sending my kids to a private school, even though we couldn't afford it.

Renting an art studio, even though I had never painted before.

Teaching yoga before becoming certified.

Going away for a seven-week yoga teacher training to become certified while I still had children living at home.

Asking Mom to move in with us.

Why did I do those things? Because on a soul level, it was the right thing to do.

Kelly and I met the summer after I graduated from high school. We were both visiting Coronado, California with friends when we started talking one night around a bonfire. His light brown wavy hair hung to his shoulders perfectly shaping his smooth face, green eyes, and lit-up smile. I was immediately attracted to him, but starting a new relationship before college was the last thing on my mind. We shared interests and stories and after three days, I knew he was the one. After falling in love with him, my life's direction changed. I wanted to move past my teenage experiences and take on the role of mature and settled adult. Being with him as he graduated and began his career became important to me. If this was the man I was going to marry, why not marry him now? At the time, being eighteen didn't seem to be a reason for holding back. People spoke about me with words like, "It's so sad," "She had such potential," and "Too bad." From my perspective, it just seemed like the next natural step.

I believe that when I am guided to make a crucial decision in my life, I am the only one I can trust. No one else lives in my body and knows how I feel or knows what persuades me to take action. I knew that our union was God-given; and this year, Kelly and I celebrated our thirtieth wedding anniversary.

Our current home once sat in complete disarray. Owned by the bank and left in a shambles, it had four-inch royal blue shag carpet throughout and harvest gold countertops. The moment I drove up the driveway and saw the view, I was breathless. I couldn't speak. All I could do was walk through the house and see the space. Its open floor plan matched our family perfectly. I knew again, without a doubt, that this house was mine. I leaned over to my real estate agent, looking at the other potential buyers and whispered, "They're in my house."

He said, "What?"

I then firmly repeated, "They're in my house." He was shocked at my instant knowing.

I asked Kelly to come see the house I chose. He took one look at it and walked out. After some convincing, he agreed that we could make an offer. The home's potential to be extraordinary seemed obvious to me. The house itself just asked to be cared for once again. I honestly felt the house's sadness in its empty and let-go state and felt a responsibility to give it back a function and a life. The views, the land, the wildlife… We converted the house into a home. After my kids grew up and moved out, the living room became my yoga studio. People enjoy the home on a daily basis and bring their joy and energy here. It is a cycle of appreciation for a home that was less than valued.

Years later, when I rented an art studio downtown with my friend Beth, questioning looks came my way. I had never been an artist, although I had always aspired to be one. Honestly, I didn't know what I would do in the space, but I did know that I needed to give myself the opportunity to find out. I began painting with acrylics and decorating wooden crosses, shelves, stools, and other items, which were happily received in the community. Knowing that my pieces of art reside in other's homes is heartwarming.

Throughout each occasion of my being unreasonable, I had the support of a knowledgeable and experienced ally. When I wished to be married, Mom gave me the peace of mind I needed, as she observed the special love that Kelly and I shared. When I wanted to buy our home, my Grandma Jere, an interior designer, saw the home's promise and encouraged me to hang in there throughout the process. When my girlfriend Beth asked me to share an art space "just for fun," I agreed. Each time I made a life-changing decision, it was extremely important to have the input and guidance from a wise, well-versed friend.

I have said "unreasonable," because at the time, others looked upon these choices as just that. But internally, I knew. On my thirteenth birthday, I traveled half way across the world to a country I knew nothing about with a group I had never met. Yet, the opportunity to spread peace at a time when peace was still practiced in Iran proved to be astounding. Financially, it was a stretch for us to put our kids into private school and to buy the home of our dreams, but once we made our decisions, the money followed. I knew that the decisions I made were good and right for me, my life, and my family. They always stretched us to a higher level of trust and paid off in a variety of abundant ways. Now I look forward to more unreasonable choices in the future.

What about you?

What do you consider unreasonable?

What have others thought unreasonable for you?

If you are not putting yourself or your family at risk, then being unreasonable deserves a second look. Basically, you're on the right track when you have the burning desire to take action, accompanied by the support of someone wise and experienced, as well as the faith, discernment, and trust to see it through. When all of these attributes line up, as well as the knowledge that most everyone else thinks you are crazy, go for it!

20

A MAGICAL RIDE

It was one day before what would have been Grandma's one-hundredth birthday, and I had been ultrasensitive to any signs and messages she might be trying to share. As I drove to meet my friend at her home, I listened to *On Broadway* on Sirius XM. "Too Many Rings around Rosie" came on. *Here we go*. Grandma was here. My black Prius switched from land vehicle to ethereal craft, transporting me along the road. "We're All in the Same Boat" followed. I laughed out loud. This song had curiously played during the times I reminisced about Mom's driving of their Dodge Monaco, and here it was again—a belted-out sign of how we continue to travel together. Somebody had a great sense of humor, and I knew exactly whose grandma that was.

While I was driving, my cell phone rang. My friend had misunderstood our set plans and had just arrived at *my* house; our wires had crossed. Happily, I turned back toward home. Now knowing that this entire mixed-up drive was Grandma-inspired, I laughed, shook my head, and enjoyed each moment. Mesmerized, I continued to listen. "From way up here, it's crystal clear. Now I'm in a whole new world with you." It was true. Grandma would one day share her "thrilling place" with me.

When I walked into my house, my waiting friend again apologized, feeling badly about the misunderstanding. "It was a Grandma intervention," I explained. "Not to worry. How else would she have taken me on a magical ride today?"

distractions, intrusions, and detours

While writing, I have had many "distractions," as people would call them. But are they distractions or focuses?

A retired husband being home all the time

Severe anemia

A hysterectomy

Hormone imbalance

Surfacing childhood fears

Feeling suppressed emotions about my high school boyfriend

Experiencing deep forgiveness for myself and others

Asking my mother to move in with us

Asking my mother to move out

These experiences did keep me from writing as often as I would have liked. And I especially found it difficult to concentrate and articulate while being anemic. Consequently, rather than feel confined and frustrated, I fully allowed myself to sit with my emotions. Huge spiritual breakthroughs far outweighed any imaginary deadline I had. Instead, it became a real opportunity to trust in the process of divine timing, in addition to the opportunity to accept all experiences as sacred gateways to love.

I did not imagine the process being so, what I then considered, backward. I believed that everything else in my life would conveniently wait until after my book was completed. Maybe seclusion works for some people, but not for me. I tend to believe that when we are exceedingly busy, we are given big-time chances to overcome big-time issues and fears in our lives.

It's almost as though God was saying, "Hey, let's get her through this now as well. She's so busy; she won't be able to argue with it as much." At least, thinking this way made it easier for me to accept. So, during these past months, I have focused on *me*, regardless of what was happening, and went with the flow instead of fighting the circumstances.

And isn't it funny when these "intrusions" come up? What makes me laugh out loud is what happens when I get stuck on what I think is important. For instance, once, while I was sitting at a quiet café and writing, a group of women suddenly began a loud, "distracting" conversation next to me. It's not rocket science, the way spirit communicates with us. Rather than getting disturbed, I stopped writing and started listening. One lady said, "We just got back from San Francisco." Her friend answered, "The last time we were there, we ate at this great Italian restaurant." Their conversation continued, "I know. Don't you just love the Palace?" The moment I think to myself, "I wish that would change. I wish she would move," or "I wish they would stop," I redirect my attention back to me. Obviously I need to change. I need to move. I need to stop.

Fun surprise images, secret messages, and fantastic tunes show up randomly: headlines in newspapers, subjects of e-mails, messages via Facebook, lyrics in songs, numbers on clocks, scenes in movies, ads in magazines, animals on my path...all are seemingly small signs, yet, when viewed from a fun-loving and accepting perspective, quite spectacular.

Life is not going to wait for the perfect opportunity to present itself. Rather, all opportunities are perfect: spending more time with my husband, correcting an ongoing health issue, releasing old patterns, setting free the past pains of my teenage life, and helping my mother in need. Who knew that all of these gifts would present themselves at this time?

I sat at the café that day, aware of the bigger picture and grateful for my awareness. A man walked past me, talking on his phone: "Hey, you called me just in time." Is someone trying to tell me something? I'm listening.

21
GRANDMA'S
MILESTONE BIRTHDAY

"Happy birthday, Grandma Rosa." One by one, my students entered the class, setting down their yoga mats. "What a great way to celebrate her." A vase of freshly cut roses from our garden, a lit white pillar candle, and a jeweled framed photo of Grandma sat on an altar in my yoga studio. Eagerness, coupled with the scent of flowers, filled the space, which exuded "special."

For the day's commemorative yoga class, I blended a musical compilation of eclectic and impactful lyrics and tunes of all genres and styles. Grandma would have enjoyed all of them. The room glistened with delight. The music cued. After a few beginning breaths in our opening dedication, I shared a few words about Grandma and what she truly meant to me:

"Today we, of course, dedicate this practice with love to Grandma Rosa, as we celebrate what would have been her hundredth birthday. Without her, none of us would be here together. She encouraged me and inspired me to practice yoga. And my practice led to my teaching, which led to my having this studio and meeting all of you. So I would heartfully like to thank her and all of our grandmothers who loved, inspired, and encouraged us along the way. For them, we are so grateful."

We folded into our first relaxing forward bend, as a violin concerto by Vivaldi filled the air. Setting the mood of the class beautifully, the music blended all of our varied energies into a sense of order. Any thoughts from outside, or inside, that were trivial and routine immediately vanished. With its serious, sharp tones, Vivaldi's symphony gained everyone's attention.

On especially significant occasions, my nervousness always seemed to surface. With Grandma's sense of humor in mind, and awareness that this may be the case, I lightened it up with Dean Martin's comedic rendition of "That's Amore." Laughter spontaneously erupted. My nerves settled down as I fell into a rhythmic ease with the music.

Then, *bam*! The energy in the room jumped, as *Glee's* Lea Michele belted out "Don't Rain on My Parade." This thrill ride of a song expressed it all—the adventure of one woman standing up to life and accepting whatever was thrown at her, emulating the Rosa spirit. A deep inhale as we raised our arms in the air, followed by an ujjayi exhale through our noses while folding into a forward bend. Our movements and our heart rates increased, as we moved in sync from pose to pose.

My motto on my business card reads, "RosaYoga—where love and yoga unite." That day, the union was tangible.

Reminiscing while teaching, I found that the melodies drew me into a trancelike memory with my grandparents, together, in San Francisco. I floated into their world as the song "On the Street Where You Live" filtered through the room. I saw images of Grandma playing card games with me in the dining room. I saw the two of us walking along Chestnut Street, window shopping. I saw Grandpa handing me the bag of bread, as we all fed the pigeons at the Palace. The musical spell transported me to that warm, familiar place I loved so much.

Earlier that morning, I had woken up with a swirl in my stomach, energy circling my chest, and visions of Grandma Rosa smiling at me. Appreciating the importance of the day, I simply lay there in bed and sent my love her way. I couldn't fall back to sleep. Actually, I didn't want to. I had been anticipating her one-hundredth birthday all year.

A momentary pause between songs. And then it started. "Just In Time," Grandma's signature song. "You found me just in time." She personified the music, then and now, and this birthday compilation would not have been complete without it. I gave it a lot of thought and decided I wanted to place this tune somewhere in the middle of the mix. The idea of ending the class with this song, as though it represented her dying, didn't seem right. "Just In Time" was a milepost on her road of life, marking just one meaningful experience of many, both before and after her passing.

I wondered if all of my students felt Grandma's presence alive in the room, just as I did. "Wherever we go, whatever we do, we're gonna go through it together." Certain of her spirit there, it continued, "Now all we need is someone with nerve…" I giggled at the innuendo. "Together wherever we go."

The "Intermezzo" from *Carmen* entered, with a seamless transition. An opera's magnetism always imbued the room with talent and culture; thus, adding it to the day's celebration just made sense. I imagined Grandma, dressed in red, performing for her ethereal audience just as Tina suggested.

Grandma Rosa's spirit complemented these songs that embodied her. The lyrics became channels for her to communicate and send well wishes; and I, too, used those same channels in return. "I give to you, and you give to me, true love, true love." Lyrics expressed more than I could do. Tears welled in my eyes, as I realized the magnitude of the day once again. Somehow existing in both worlds, I continued to teach, knowing our guardian angels watched over us, loved us, and created the opening for us to love each other. I imagined Grandma next to me, holding me and leaving no space between us.

a gift of nonperfection

Today I bestow upon you a "Gift of Nonperfection." The box containing this gift comes with no strings attached and can be redeemed every day for the rest of your life. It comes complete with an open mind, easygoing attitude, and an infinite amount of possibilities.

To use, simply leave your "ideals" on the table and begin by closing your mouth during conversations, letting go of the ego that needs to speak up at all times and to have the last word. Instead, listen. You will hear many happier, if imperfect, conversations.

If you need to look "wiser," then this gift is for you. No man is ever wiser than the silent one, who assimilates information and then speaks only words of meaning and thoughtfulness. Those who are too quick-witted only shine the spotlight on themselves, and it is that same spotlight that exposes their most pronounced flaws. This inevitably takes perfectionists to their knees, which is where they will find all of their friends and family. A more jovial place than the once grand pedestal that can only hold one—with no room for growth, joy, or others.

To get the most out of this gift, sprinkle the "Packet of Humor" all over your body, from head to toe. As it lands and becomes absorbed into your skin, you will find that this path of imperfection is a delight—full of laughter and lightheartedness for you and all those you come into contact with.

You will be the one people laugh at and with, so enjoy the theoretical refrigerator magnet, stating our Imperfect Motto: "It Just Doesn't Matter." Repeat this motto again and again, until it becomes a natural response at any given time. "It just doesn't matter. It just doesn't matter. It just doesn't matter." These four words will pave the way into your new world.

Directions for beginners:

Step 1. Wear clothes that don't match.

Step 2. Allow a friend to come over while there are still dirty dishes in the sink.

Step 3. One day this week, don't make your bed.

Step 4. The next time you think, "I should...," change it to "I don't have to..."

Ultimately, you will want to take on the thinking pattern that everyone else is right and you are wrong. Be careful. This is not meant to lower your self-image in a negative way. It is simply meant to lower your self-image...knock it down a notch or two... or a hundred. The self you will find on this path is no different than the self you will see and hear and know in others. This same self is your ticket to freedom. Once you realize this, your contentment will grow greater, and your time here will be more satisfying.

Now that you are on your way to imperfectionism, write down any amusing changes, and share them with your closest supporters. Take out the "Key to Joy" and unlock the window that has now opened up a greater view of your authentic existence. You will notice a new regard for the Earth, animals, water, and sky. Willing to move out of your own way, you can now admire and be grateful for so much more of the world around you.

The sign reading "Love and Gratitude for All" is to be placed at your bedside as a constant reminder of your gift. Every morning when you first wake up, and each night before you go to sleep, recall all of the day's moments, feeling love and gratitude for each one of them. Make sure you include the "difficult" experiences as well, because every opportunity to grow and become more imperfect is a big part of this original gift.

Finally, ask for help. Anyone who has been bestowed this amazing reward has also been given a "HELP" card that never expires and is redeemable in any language, on any planet, and at any time. This "HELP" card is attached to many forms of energy that are waiting to assist you. To activate their assistance, simply ask.

Thank you for receiving this "Gift of Nonperfection," as I know it will bring you many fun-filled, awe-inspiring tours along the way.

22

THE BIG REVEAL

Today my daughter Kristina called with the great news. *"You are going to be a grandmother!"* Visions of grandma-possibilities popped up like a slide show in my head. Playing card games, reading children stories, singing show tunes, finding secret treasures, taking nature walks. In my mind, I closed my eyes and saw Grandma passing me a gold baton, saying, "Now it's your turn to run with it." I thought, *how amazing is it that I get to be the grandma now. I would be an awesome grandma.*

Our first gathering took place at the obstetrician's office on the day we would find out whether this new baby was a boy or a girl. Doctor Hutchison grinned and asked, "Are you ready?" She is one of those rare doctors who give hugs on your first visit and makes you feel as though you are the most important patient she has. "Your baby is going to be the most beautiful baby ever," she told Levi, my son-in-law. "This is so exciting," she added enthusiastically, as though this were her first time working the ultrasound machine. Levi's mother, Diane, and I crowded into the small checkup room with our kids, awaiting the news of our soon-to-be grandbaby.

I watched as she squeezed a pile of gel on Kristina's tummy and smiled. "Here we go," she said.

The first image showed the smooth round shape of the baby's head. She saw the soft curves of the body, listened to the rapid heartbeat, and ruled out potential complications. Then we saw a perfect foot, an open hand, an amazing spine, each a picture of health and beauty. "OK, now look away." We all turned around, including Kristina and Levi, facing away from the monitor. "Okay."

Diane immediately asked, "Did you see? Could you tell if it was a boy or a girl?"

The doctor beamed with bright eyes. "Yes, I could." The energy in the room sparkled. Excitedly, we paced about as she finished. Doctor Hutchison left us and walked into her office to cut the gender-specific images out of the photo strip. She wrote the findings down on a piece of paper and sealed it in an envelope.

After the appointment, Kristina and Levi delivered the baby news to the cake bakery. The women bakers rushed to the back, giggling as they opened the envelope. Only they and the doctor knew the sex of the baby. We had called the bakery earlier that week to place the order for the "big reveal" cake. Instructions were that the cake would need to be frosted on the day of the obstetrician appointment, *after* the doctor discovered whether Kristina and Levi were having a boy or a girl. Either blue or pink frosting would fill the center layers, showing everyone at the celebration the gender of their new baby. "Boy or Girl?" with a great big question mark, was written across the top of the cake, in equally divided blue and pink lettering.

As the sun was setting, our families met at the kids' house. Our enthusiasm was palpable. In the background, Kelly chanted, "Girl! Girl! Girl! Girl!" He had been hoping for a girl from the beginning.

Tears rolled down Kristina's cheeks even before she cut the cake, and she said, "Thank you all for being here and sharing in this moment with us." It's so great when she cries. It is such an honest and real emotion for her—not one that happens often or just because. When Kristina cries, everyone cries. With hearts racing, they began.

She and Levi each held a knife and, pressing the two tips together, sliced down the center, cutting the first piece of cake. With one plate in hand and a spatula underneath, they paused. Clapping erupted, followed by silence. Slowly, they lifted up the piece—instantaneous cheering rose with it.

Beautiful soft pink layers. The elevation of elation exploded. Screams shot out, "Girl! Girl! It's a Girl!" We celebrated with family members and others, who were listening on cell phones, all united there. Kristina and Levi cried, kissed, and hugged.

Luminous love radiated as that first piece was cut. Obviously, the women at the bakery had smiled and spread their joy into the frosted layers. The pink cream was so tall that I knew they were especially conscious of making it easy for each person at home to see. "A name…Do you have a name?" Levi's mom exclaimed. Kristina and Levi gave each other a gentle look, as if to say, "We have known who she was all along." Realizing their delight of a new baby daughter, they spoke: "Ellis Rose."

The instant they said her name aloud, she imprinted her stamp on each of our hearts. Images of holding her and rocking her and loving her rushed into my mind. My body filled with overwhelming and complete joy, head to toe. Ellis and I would have many magnificent grandmother-granddaughter moments together. And Grandma is surely smiling and singing, excited for a new Rose to love.

No doubt the energy of the entire neighborhood changed that night, simply because of our elevated vibration. Sharing this dynamic occasion as one family, for one singular second, was extraordinary. I imagined parties like this happening everywhere now. Neighborhoods lighting up with joyous love and laughter. Yes, maybe that's it. All we need are more reasons for cake.

I'm listening...

After one of her baby showers, Kristina sent out thank-you notes. On the front of the card, were toy blocks with the letters T, H, A, N, K, and S on them. They looked as though they were falling from the top of the note, floating in the air. Below were only two other blocks, with the letters E and Q. The rest of the design blended in.

Courtney called Kristina and asked, "Where did you order the special note cards?" Kristina told her that they were simply in a box of fifty on the shelf at the store. They weren't specially ordered. "Why?" Kristina asked.

"Because they have Ellis's initials on them...T H A N K S...E. Q. Ellis Quesada."

divine time

Celebrating and welcoming a new baby into this world is just as astounding as witnessing the passing on of a loved one. Being present for those moments where love is arriving and departing this world are equally miraculous. Precious times make grand impacts on fascinated souls like me.

It is as though the physical human self is set aside; and in its place, the soul exists and is exposed openly. I imagine it looking like a bursting white light, surging out from the heart's center into the universe, nullifying all other external energy while creating a safe enclosure. The body becomes cocooned in a temporary bath of light, surrounding us and protecting us from all outside activities, noises, and conflicts. And I imagine that with such an astonishing amount of love bursting from the heart, all of the other senses deaden, leaving the body motionless and still.

Altogether, the sensation is one of stopping time.

Such love unlocks the mind from its repetitive thought patterns and spurs it to radical expansion—open to all feelings, emotions, and concepts. Thoughts become clear. Emotions become full and profound. The spirit ignites and tingles with questions. It's a fireworks finale of information—that space where all intuition and knowledge become available.

It is at this moment when we get a clearer picture of true time. Not in the sense of a second, minute, or hour. Only in the sense of *one*. One person, one life, one memory, one relationship, one moment, one heart, one soul. All of this in one divine time.

Have you ever felt motionless in time?

How did it feel, and what did that moment reveal to you?

Have you experienced a time when all things came together in perfect union? In divine time?

23

ELLIS ROSE

There aren't words to describe the joy and bliss one feels as a new grandparent. For me, knowing the opportunity to say "I love you" and sing in public to my granddaughter was beyond magical. Ellis Rose was born one week ago weighing six pounds, seven ounces. Beautiful brown hair, deep brown eyes, and gorgeous pink skin. Our world was complete.

After her first week checkup, Kristina called. "Mom, can you come over?" she asked.

"Is everything OK?" I asked.

"The doctor says Ellis has cystic fibrosis."

All I could think of saying was, "Why?" I guess I just didn't understand how they could know so soon, without a family history of CF. She looked and acted like such a healthy baby girl.

"The test from the infant screening came back positive," Kristina tearfully muttered.

I stopped working. "I'm on my way."

I chose silence over music and arrived to an even deeper silence at their home. Kristina lay in bed, holding Ellis. Without thinking, I calmly climbed in next to her and pulled up the covers. Together we cried and stared at our jewel of a sweetheart. Levi quietly walked in, paused for a moment, and then climbed into bed on the other side of Kristina. One never knows what to say or how to behave in these circumstances. Sometimes silence says more than words. So I surrendered to just being with them. I said and did nothing. We just cried.

Ironically, at home, flyers sat next to my yoga sign-in book, asking people to donate used items to a huge rummage sale for CF. One of my student's granddaughters has the disease, and she had asked me if she could leave them there for others. I, of course, obliged. The week before Ellis arrived, Kristina and Levi had set out a pile of linens, bags of clothing, and kitchen items to get rid of, to make room for all of the new baby-related paraphernalia. I, too, felt the nesting instinct and had gone through my closet, gathering the items I hadn't been using and didn't need. I placed the bags and boxes in the backseat of my car for the sale. They sat there now, as I lay inside with my children.

This cause was now our cause.

It took us two days to deal with our shock and anger and the unimaginable revelation from the diagnosis. But that was it. From that day on, I decided that our family would not partake in the doom and gloom of a disease but rather cherish the moments and love of our little Ellis, just as we would if she didn't have CF. Together, we have done just that.

We know that Ellis has a profound purpose, and we are grateful that she chose our family to support her and to grow with her. We feel honored to share in whatever story she needs to tell and know that her life is surrounded and filled with amazing love and wisdom. I never would have thought it possible that our family could become even closer than before, but thanks to Ellis, we feel more, love greater, and thank often. She has obviously already stepped into the role of great teacher for us all.

I'm listening...

After getting into the car and driving home from Kristina's house on the day of the diagnosis, I listened to the *On Broadway* channel on XM radio and heard the host, Christine Pedi, talk about one of her favorite ushers at a theater in New York City. "Rose has been there for as long as I can remember," she said. "I love stopping by the theater to say 'hello' from time to time. She always has a way of lifting me up when I am feeling sad and making me smile." She followed with her Rose-inspired song, "Always Look on the Bright Side of Life," from the show *Spamalot*.

"Really, Grandma...really? It's a little too soon, don't you think?" Aloud I looked up to the sky and admitted that anger and concern and disbelief had my full attention. Hearing news of such degree and shock left me stinging. I wasn't exactly sure how I would work through these feelings until the next night's dream:

> I am swimming in a pool, holding long serrated knives, cutting through the water with each stroke. Nobody in the pool seems to be surprised or nervous. They simply watch me from above or move to the side of the pool so I can pass. With each stroke, I feel the anger begin to subside. I do a flip turn, with my knives still in hand. A few laps later, my anger dissolves even more. Once calm, I get out of the pool and towel off. I look over at the line of chairs and other people's belongings and notice personalized carrying cases for the knives *they* brought to swim with that day.

I woke up feeling relieved and serene after "cutting through my emotions."

Later that week, we read about a new drug coming out on the market. It will alleviate the lung infections, sticky mucus, and high chloride levels patients deal with. This drug helps 4 percent of the CF population who have a specific gene—G551D. Ellis is one of those people.

i choose peace

"What are you going to do now?"

I ask myself this question every time life places turbulence in front of me. A broken dishwasher, a rude driver, an unnecessary lecture…Am I going to keep my peace, or give it away? Dogs barking, dirty footsteps down the hall, a long line…How about now? What am I going to do now?

Today I choose peace. I haven't always made such choices. There were times when the warning went off inside me, and I knew that my soon-to-be-chosen remark or action would carry pain and anguish with it. I would hear that voice, that whisper of guidance, but would think *I don't need to listen. I am in control. I know what I am doing.*

Back then I would go ahead and make that remark or call that friend at just the wrong time. On each occasion, when I got caught up in the illusion of "I don't need help," or "I can do this alone," my life got out of sync. Somewhere inside my human self, I actually *desired* misery. I played into the drama, adding my own words and stories to it. I believed that suffering was part of life and that I had no control over it. And I believed that everyone experienced that same internal war with themselves.

Today I am different. Now, minute by minute, second by second, I check in with my heart to notice and connect to that feeling of peace—that feeling of complete honesty, sincerity, and acceptance.

With my yoga practice, conscious breathing, facing of fears, and letting go of "shoulds," I am able to trust "what is" rather than "what ought to be." I have worked diligently at keeping my serenity. Anytime I feel the urge to boast or criticize, I catch myself and immediately challenge my thinking: *Is that true?* I practice keeping my emotions even-keeled and my ego in check, witnessing each situation from an observer's perspective. What is there to learn now? What is the bigger picture? What has happened to create this, and why?

We are surrounded completely and overwhelmingly by love.
As we learn to take care of ourselves, our self's take care of us.
And once connected to that energy, the true self emerges—one
of peace.

What does peace mean to you?

How do you feel when you choose peace?

Do you listen to your inner voice, guardian angels, and guides
and ask for help?

I'm listening...

While meditating, I heard, "Choice."
I asked God, "Is there anything else?"
I heard, "Make one."

24

THE MUSIC PLAYED ON

After Grandma passed, the music continued to fill the hospital room with sweet, harmonious lyrics. "Together, wherever we go." Because there were no machines connected to Grandma, the room stayed private; we were the only ones aware of her last breath and the only ones surrounding her bed. After a long drum roll and single crash on a cymbal: "What good is sitting alone in your room, come hear the music play. Life is a cabaret..." We stood by Grandma, allowing the moment the precious time it deserved. Listening and feeling all the human responses that rise at death, we immersed ourselves in the music. "Start by admitting, from cradle to tomb, isn't that long a stay. Life is a cabaret..."

Shaking our heads and smiling, we remained in awe. "The Music of the Night" spread grace and peace into the already blessed space. Its dynamic orchestration moved our souls and strummed our heartstrings. Our bodies pulsed with an overwhelming desire to simply stand still and receive this holy experience.

"Kiss today good-bye, the sweetness and the sorrow." Her spirit continued to share a dying message from her. "Wish me luck the same to you. But I can't regret what I did for love…what I did for love." We stood silently by her side, taking it all in. "Look, my eyes are dry. The gift was ours to borrow." Life is truly precious, and living is an honor. Brilliant music continued to fill the air, each expression a gem, one amplifying the other.

"Gone, love is never gone. As we travel on, love's what we'll remember." And isn't this true in life? Love, alone, is the reason for living. Grandma welcomed her next journey without regret, in love with every moment.

showing up

Recently, I won the grand prize at a raffle: a spa day for two at Canyon Ranch, a world premier health resort here in Tucson. The people standing around me couldn't believe that I won, out of so many entries. "I never win anything," one friend stated. I asked her how many tickets she bought. She said, "None." As the saying goes, "You can't win if you don't play." Great opportunities don't happen without your permission and participation.

My retelling of Grandma's life stories and of my relationship with her, although relayed with deep meaning, can never be as powerful or as miraculous as being there. My viewpoint and rendition of her story may be precise, but it is still only a best attempt at sharing the deep feelings and emotional significance it had for me. Being with Grandma throughout her life, even when her moods changed, her body depleted, and her mind wandered, gave me a reason to live, to love, and to go out and show up for more.

In those unique moments of "choice," time is happily supportive. Choose to be a part of all of life's mysteries. For me, Grandma's dying was enough to make time stand still. And as she lived "just in time," so did she die. It was beautiful beyond words.

I believe it helps to articulate the details of important occurrences as a way to give tribute and honor the moment, so it is not only sensed with feeling and remembered by thought, but also sensed and remembered with words. There are so many ways to consecrate the extraordinary events of a person's life. Paint a picture, write a song, say a prayer. Yet, the best things in life happen when you are there, so show up!

I'm listening...

After leaving the hospital, we walked into the house with a "What do we do now?" haze over us. Slowly, we took action. Mom called the Neptune Society, which handled all of Grandma's cremation plans. I began to write the obituary, documenting all of the names of family and relatives. JoAnn made some personal phone calls, informing others of Grandma's death. Together we took care of the details. Grandma had done her part, also. All of the arrangements had been made, her finances left in order, family heirlooms passed down, and clothing donated.

That afternoon, we stopped by the care home, where she had been living. Mom said, "I'll just be a minute." I asked her if I could help, and she said, "No, I've got it." She came out of the home, carrying two plastic bags in her hands.

"That's it?" I asked.

"This is everything," she answered.

"But that was so easy." I replied.

EPILOGUE

This book is not so much about the incredible relationship that Grandma and I shared, but about the experiences themselves which transform us, teaching us new ways to grow. Our story is not meant to act as a comparison to your own, yet meant to offer you an opportunity to reflect upon your own life, your own relationships, and your own journey. If her love, her enthusiasm, and her joy of living excite you, ignite you, and inspire you to live in a new way, then anyone can be your guide. A rose by any other name…

Grandma Rosa Moore at The Palace of Fine Arts
August, 1986

GRANDMA'S MUSICAL PLAYLIST

Bernstein, Leonard, Adolph Green, and Betty Comden. "New York, New York." *On the Town*. 1944. CD

Caesar, Irving, Otto Harbach, and Vincent Youmans. "Too Many Rings Around Rosie." *No, No, Nanette.*, 1940. CD

Fatboy Slim, "Because We Can." *Moulin Rouge!* 2001. CD

Kander, John, and Ralph Burns. "Cabaret." *Cabaret*. 1972. CD

Kane, Brad. "A Whole New World." *Aladdin*. 1991. CD

Kleban, Edward, and Marvin Hamlisch. "Kiss Today Good-bye." *A Chorus Line*. 1975. CD

Loesser, Frank. "The Most Happy Fella." *The Most Happy Fella*. 1956. CD

Rodgers, Mary, and Marshall Barer. "Shy." *Once Upon a Mattress.*
1959. CD

Rodgers, Mary, and Marshall Barer. "The Swamps of Home."
Once Upon a Mattress. 1959. CD

Rogers, Richard, and Oscar Hammerstein II. "Getting To Know
You." *The King and I.* 1951. CD

Rogers, Richard, and Oscar Hammerstein II. "Oklahoma!"
Oklahoma! 1943. CD

Sigmund Romberg, Sigmund, Leo Robin, and Jeanmaire and
Charles Goldner. "We're All In the Same Boat." *The Girl in
Pink Tights.* 1954. CD

Styne, Jule, and Stephen Sondheim. "Together (Wherever We
Go)." *Gypsy.* 1959. CD

Styne, Jule, Betty Comden, and Adolph Green. "Just In Time."
Bells Are Ringing. 1956. CD

Williams, John. "The Music of the Night." *Phantom of the Opera.*
Boston Pops Orchestra, 1990. CD

BOOK CLUB CONVERSATIONS

1. What does the word *joy* mean to you? Is it a feeling or a knowing? Or both? Share an example of what it means to live joyfully.

2. Are you feeling "stuck?" What areas of your life feel out of balance? What small step can you make towards bringing balance back into your life?

3. We all experience "universal time-outs;" those events that stop our routines or break our patterns. What "universal time-out" have you experienced and how did that *time* change the direction of your life?

4. Do you ever catch yourself saying phrases like "I'm just wasting time" or "I have time to kill?" How can you open your awareness and change your perspective to having "time to spend" and "time to just be?"

5. Share a song, symbol, or sign that occurred in your life and opened your heart to love.

6. Share an experience that you have felt all alone in. Once shared out loud, you will truly understand that "we are all in the same boat."

7. What fear are you ready and willing to face? How can you take a small step in a fearless direction? Is there anyone you can ask who might want to join you on your adventure? Camaraderie is always a good way to go.

8. What can you celebrate today? Not because it is your birthday or anniversary. Those are givens. But a celebration of other sorts. A celebration of listening to your spirit and following its guidance and wisdom. Make a list of ten things you can celebrate and then share with the group. Keep adding to the list as you hear other fabulous ideas and then take action every day to enjoy YOU!

Ten percent of all proceeds from this book will be donated to
The Cystic Fibrosis Foundation
Visit Cff.org and
Change someone's life.

ABOUT THE AUTHOR

Owner of RosaYoga since 2003, Karen Rose Callan is an E-RYT 500 yoga teacher who has taught thousands of classes, camps and workshops across the country. She and her husband, Kelly, share ownership of The Parlour Frozen Yogurt Store in Tucson, Arizona where they showcase local artists and vendors. Karen is a writer, teacher, painter, nature lover, orchid grower, and Broadway musical enthusiast. Mother of four, grandmother of two, she and Kelly share their time between their homes in Tucson and Sedona, Arizona with their adored four-legged friends, Clay and Chloe. For more information, please visit www.rosayoga.com or www.facebook.com/JustinTimeByKarenRoseCallan

CPSIA information can be obtained at www.ICGtesting.com
Printed in the USA
LVOW12s2223220514

387024LV00011B/147/P